401 (not) OK

James L. Beattey

Acknowledgments

I have the great privilege of working with a fantastic group of financial professionals all over the country who are committed to being informed, client-oriented, and solutions-focused. Each of you inspire and motivate me to continue providing tools and information to help you carry our very important message to the public.

I also work with a wonderful group of staff and business partners who keep me on point and constantly remind me that ours is a crusade that requires diligence, tireless effort, and clarity of purpose.
Thank you Dave, Luci, and Julie.

The <u>Absence</u> of knowledge is <u>Enslavement</u>.
The <u>Possession</u> of knowledge is <u>Enlightenment</u>.
The <u>Application</u> of Knowledge is <u>Liberating!</u>

Beattey, 2017

Table of Contents

Part 2: The Alternative...

Definitions

To save trees (and ink), I'll be referring throughout this book to the '401k.' What I really mean (and just don't want to write a thousand times) is not just the 401k, but all its cousins, the 403b, 457, IRA, SEP, SIMPLE, and a few others.

All these so-called 'tax-qualified' plans were established by the government in the 1970's. While there are nuanced differences between them, they share a common set of characteristics – namely:

- The ability to make pre-tax contributions

- The ability to grow money tax-deferred

While not a feature of all plans, many employers 'match' a portion of the employee contributions.

What you'll learn in these pages applies to almost all of them – the exceptions being the "Roth" versions of these plans. Roth plans overcome some of the deficiencies of 'traditional' plans, but still share many characteristics in common (we'll make the distinctions later).

As you read '401k' in the pages that follow – know that I'm referring to all of these plans collectively – most likely including yours.

Foreword

have two very smart and beautiful daughters. Both landed nice jobs with nationally known firms out of college and are off to great starts in their lives.

Their 'new employee orientation' was probably a lot like yours – papers being shoved at them with a sentence or two of explanation – in the expectation that they'd make quick decisions, sign on the dotted line, and get to work.

Both were introduced to their company's respective 401k plans. They were told how the company would match a portion of any contributions they made to the plan. Their contributions would be made 'pre-tax' (meaning they'd have fewer taxes taken from their paychecks), and their money would grow tax-deferred until they retired.

What a deal. Free money from their employers – a 'subsidy' from Uncle Sam – and their companies would surely give them investment options that were best for them and the company's other employees – right?

Such has been the American story since the advent of the 401k and most of the other tax-qualified plans in the 1970's. For the most part, they've served more than a generation of Americans reasonably well, but their role has changed dramatically over that time.

Qualified plans were intended to be the third leg of a three-legged retirement stool anchored by employer-funded pensions - and Social Security. But as employers realized they could replace their high-cost, high-risk pension plans with less expensive 401k plans, pensions began to quickly go the way of the dinosaur.

Today, very few traditional pension plans remain in the private sector, and that three-legged stool is (mostly) two-legged; with one of those legs - Social Security – rather termite-infested, and looking more than a bit wobbly.

The net result is that the 401k is now the *foundation* of most retirement plans rather than a *supplement* to the others.

Pension plans are typically constructed as 'defined benefit' plans. They 'define' a retiree's lifetime income benefit. With these plans, <u>employers</u> take on:

- The *funding risk* - the risk that they're putting enough money that, when wisely invested, there is enough to pay the plan's promised benefit

- The *investment risk* - the risk that they are investing their money wisely enough to cover the retiree's benefit, and

- The *longevity risk* - the risk that there will be enough money to continue paying retirees who live well beyond their life expectancy.

With the advent of the 401k – <u>all three of these risks</u> shift to the employee = who must now additionally concern themselves with things like cooperative markets – buying the right kinds of investments – diversification – portfolio balance – market timing – running out of money – or myriad other factors that will directly influence their retirement paycheck.

The result is nothing short of a national **retirement crisis**. According to a 2015 Government Accountability Office study, 29% of Americans 55 and older don't have *any* retirement nest egg or traditional pension plan. Those who do have retirement funds don't have enough money: 55 to 64-year-olds have an average of $104,000 and those 65 to 74 have $148,000 in savings.

If that money were turned into lifetime income, it would only amount to $310 and $649 per month, respectively - not nearly enough to sustain even a modest lifestyle. To the extent Americans rely on the 401k to add to these paltry sums, employees:

- Procrastinate, save less, and save later,

- Have no idea how much retirement income they can count on,

- Are clueless about how much they need to be saving to achieve a particular income figure,

- Live every day both exposed to risk of loss and live in fear of financial markets,

- Have to become educated on what investments to purchase and hold in their accounts,

- Have no idea when they can safely/comfortably retire,

- Are oblivious to what their future tax-liability will be, and

- Must 'time' retirement to avoid getting 'caught' by an uncooperative market (think of those who were ready to retire in 2008 when the market took a 40% dump)

These are issues that now – even 40 years after the first qualified retirement plans came into existence – we don't teach, we don't give much attention to, and as a result, we don't manage very well. Some do of course, but on the whole, there are far more horror stories than there are success stories when it comes to Americans, retirement, and the 401k.

Unfortunately, the pitfalls of the 401k don't end at the tidy little list we just looked at. The law of unintended consequences has been working overtime in 401k-land, and the goal of this volume is to share those with you.

It will get more depressing before it gets better – but it will get better! Because in the late 90's, another kind of plan emerged. This one from private industry. And it is a far better plan for many Americans – perhaps including you. You'll learn about it in detail in the pages that follow.

Thankfully, a small but growing army of trained professionals can help you learn about and understand this plan. Its gaining credibility among pundits, and is achieving traction in the marketplace. Every day, thousands of Americans are abandoning the worn-out 401k, and taking control over their financial futures in a new way.

But getting good information into the hands of the public has been a challenge. The industry offering this new kind of plan is not as well organized or funded as the entrenched Wall Street Cartel that advocates for the 401k. The stakes are so high that the Wall Streeters' *'defend the status quo at all cost'* effort requires investors to dig deep and peel the onion back to even learn about this alternative.

But you're here. And while the story your about to embark on is like that of David and Goliath, it is real. It's true. And it's important for you to know.

It will require of you however, a level of open-mindedness that will be challenging. What you're about to learn will fly in the face of what you've been taught and what has been reinforced by institutions and people you have come to trust — even love. But the reward for those who remain diligent is the kind of reliable, stress-free retirement you envisioned when you made the commitment to start saving for tomorrow in the first place.

We'll make the case for this new alternative so you can decide for yourself whether it could represent a better path for you and your family. But first, I want you to know just how bad the 401k is — and I'm going to make the point by detailing…

…the 16 things you agreed to (unknowingly), when you signed up for the company 401k plan?

Get   ready: Truth   Journey,   ahead!'

Part 1

401 (not) Ok

'I Want to Be Deceived by Mathematical Trickery'

While some employers offer 401k plan participants 'matching' contributions,' the two universal benefits touted by those who promote the 401k are:

1. The ability to make pre-tax contributions, and
2. The benefit of tax-deferred growth

Seems logical. Who wouldn't want to save money before taxes were taken out? And who wouldn't want to defer paying taxes on that money – as well as the growth on that money – until sometime down the road?

But what if you discovered that there really was <u>no benefit to pre-tax contributions or tax-deferred growth</u> at all?

What if it was all a big marketing lie to lure you into the 401k lair where you would be trapped forever – unless of course you were willing to pay an extra toll to get yourself out of your predicament?

It *is* a lie – and a cruel one at that. To understand how the deception is perpetrated, we'll use a financial shortcut called the 'rule of 72.'

The rule explains the power of compound interest - which Albert Einstein calls the 9th Wonder of the World. It's rather simple. Dividing the number 72 by an interest rate tells us how long it will take to double a sum of money.

- If we divide 72 by an interest rate of 7.2%, we'll double our money in 10 years.

- Likewise, 72 divided by an interest rate of 10% tells us that at 10% - we'll double our money in 7.2 years. Get it?

So, let's put it to work to reveal this math trick.

	Pre-Tax (401k)	After-tax (25% tax rate)
Beginning Balance	$1,000	$750
Balance in 10 years @ 7.2%	$2,000	$1,500
Tax Liability (assume 25% tax rate)	($500)	-0-
Net Available	$1,500	$1,500

A $1,000 pretax contribution will double to $2,000 in 10 years if it grows at 7.2%. If we saved after-tax dollars instead – the same $1,000 will leave us with only $750 to invest after taxes (assuming a 25% tax rate). At the same 7.2% growth rate – over the same 10 years – our $750 would also double to $1,500.

Even a second grader knows that $2,000 is more than $1,500. But that's where the Wall Street story abruptly ends.

The real story has one more important chapter. To get the $2,000 out of the 401k or other qualified plan so that it can be used to buy something, we must pay taxes on it.

At the same 25% tax rate – we end up with – guess what - the exact same $1,500 we would have had in our after-tax account.

See, there is no mathematical advantage to pre-tax contributions or tax-deferred growth. Zip – Zero – Nada – when there is an alternative that allows us to invest after-tax dollars which are then accessible tax free – which there is!

I'm pretty sure they never told you that one when they were dangling the 401k in front of you.

Perhaps however, they told you that you'd likely be in a lower tax bracket in retirement which would give the nod to the 401k. But your retirement tax bracket can only be lower if:

1) Your income in retirement is lower, and/or

2) Future tax rates are lower

Now who wants to resign themselves to the proposition that their income will necessarily be lower in retirement? *"Hey – good news – your taxes in retirement will be lower because your income will be squat!"*

Don't you want your income to be as high as it can be? Don't you want to live out all those dreams you put off during your working years?

And even if your income is lower, chances are you won't be in a lower tax bracket – for two realistic reasons. First, you won't have as many tax deductions. There are no kids to deduct; little (if any) mortgage interest to deduct; etc. In fact, you <u>could</u> end up finding yourself in a <u>*higher*</u> tax bracket in retirement - on <u>*lower*</u> income.

Second, do you really think for a moment that tax rates will be lower when you retire? America is more than $20 trillion in debt, with another $120 trillion in unfunded liabilities – and that doesn't count the financial condition of our states and municipalities.

There are only two ways to solve that problem. <u>Spend less</u> – or <u>tax more</u>. Given what you know about Congress and our government, which do you think is the more likely path? Hint: We haven't run out of rich people to tax quite yet.

The problem is – you may find yourself labeled 'rich' by the government's definition! As you'll learn shortly, you may already be 'rich' in government-speak.

The mere fact that we must speculate on the unknowability of future tax rates proves one other point – that 401k owners will live with <u>'tax-rate-risk'</u> the rest of their lives. By investing after-tax dollars that are accessible tax-free instead, you can take tax-rate risk completely off the table – forever.

Bottom line: There is no mathematical advantage to pre-tax contributions or tax-deferred growth. It's a Wall Street mirage – it looks real, but it's mathematical sleight-of-hand – and nearly perfect 'bait' to lure Americans into an almost inescapable   financial   trap.

'I Want to Be in an Open-Ended Partnership with No Vote'

How much do you have in your 401k right now? Go ahead - grab your statement – I'll wait. It's a bit of a trick question with the operative part being, 'how much do _you_ have?'

Because you don't have the $128,562 that your statement suggests you have (or whatever figure is on your statement). Why? Baked into that number is your 'deferred tax liability.' Since not a penny of that money has been taxed you cannot take it out without paying Uncle Sam. All you know is that you have something less than $128,562. How much less is a matter of what tax rate will apply when you take it out – which we just agreed was unknowable.

How does it feel to look at that 401k statement knowing you have no idea how much of the money in that account is yours?

How does it feel to know that you'll NEVER know how much is yours?

How does it feel to know that your partner (Uncle Sam) can – with the stroke of a pen – change his share – without even asking you?

How does it feel to know that when the balance passes to your heirs you'll still never know how much they end up with –not just because you're gone – but because of how the remainder will be taxed when it passes to your heirs?

The sobering reality is that when you signed up for that tax-qualified plan, you entered into a business partnership – a partnership with the government. You may not have thought about it that way until this very moment – but that's the truth. And the terms of the partnership you agreed to are these:

- You put up all the money,

- You take all the risk,

- When you die, retire, or decide you need the money, your partner steps in to declare his share of the partnership spoils – which he will confiscate under force of law, and

- When it comes to determining what his share will be, you have no say in the matter.

There is not another area of your life where you would knowingly enter a partnership under such terms. Yet you're in this one. You were lured into that partnership by the Wall Street Cartel – the government - the Wall Street bankers - even your employer is (unwittingly) part of the scheme that sold you this rotten bill of goods.

'I Want to Pay the Highest Fees and Commissions Possible'

Some of you will be tempted to skip this chapter. You'll say to yourself, "I don't pay anything to participate in the company's 401k plan."

I've got bad news for you — you do. In fact, as we unpack our discussion of the impact of fees and commissions, there are really three important takeaways to understand:

1. **The impact of fees over a lifetime is greater than you appreciate** — no matter what kind of account you save your money in,

2. The rate of fees and commissions **you're paying is much higher than you're being told**, and

3. **401k and other qualified plan owners pay the highest rate of fees and commissions possible**.

I can see that raised eyebrow of skepticism on your face — so let's dive in.

Impact of Fees/Commissions

Whether you gather your nuts in a 401k or a non-qualified plan, the lifetime impact of fees and commissions is perhaps the <u>most underestimated of all the factors that will determine your outcome</u>. They may seem small and harmless – but so do termites!

Consider the following simple example.

Amount Saved per Month	$300	$300
Starting Age	25	25
Retirement Age	67	67
Growth Rate of Money	7.0%	7.0%
Rate of Fees & Commissions	1%	2%
Principal at Retirement	$681,048	$513,405
Retirement Income	$27,242	$20,536

The only difference between the columns is the rate of fees and commissions taken from the respective accounts. The first column shows a 1% fee drain, the second column, 2%.

Could you ever have guessed that a tiny 1% difference in fees and commissions could mean 25% less income in retirement?

It doesn't matter what numbers you plug into the formula, the proportionality of the impact remains the same, and makes the point – that <u>we grossly underestimate the impact of fees and commissions on our money</u>.

Whether you stay with the 401k or adopt the alternative solution you'll meet a bit later, you should now be sufficiently motivated to much more closely scrutinize what you pay in fees and commissions – and do some shopping and negotiating.

The money you're saving and investing is supposed to be making YOU wealthy – not the Wall Street cartel!

You're paying more than you think you are

In the example we just used, we compared a 1% fee and commission account to a 2% fee and commission account. You're probably paying far more than either number – and that should be frightening.

There are two categories of cost inside a qualified plan like a 401k. There are costs to set up and administer the plan itself. These costs are called **Plan Fees** and must be disclosed by law. As such, they can be easily researched by either asking your employer for a summary plan document, or by searching online for the company's 'form 5500' which is a public record.

Some employers deduct the plan's costs from the plan's assets (meaning your money). Some bear the cost themselves; and others share the costs with the plan participants in some proportion (you – again).

Because plans can be so different one to the next, we won't dwell on which type of cost arrangement applies to your plan. What *is* worth focusing on however, are the costs related to the securities held in your account. Those costs are born by you – 100% - in all cases.

While 401ks typically offer a menu of investment options, they're usually heavily weighted toward mutual funds. But mutual funds are riddled with fees and costs – the majority of which are unseen even though you're paying them anyway.

The most obvious (and the one that is published by law) is the fund's **expense ratio**. This is essentially the fund operator's annual budget for its costs of operating and administering the plan. The expense ratio is stated as a percentage of the fund's assets deducted annually - and can range from less than ½% up to 2% or more.

According to Morningstar – a mutual fund reporting service, the average mutual fund expense ratio is 1.25% per year. Knowing now what the impact of a 1% *differential* in net return means, you can better appreciate why shopping and comparing fund expenses can have a dramatic effect on your investing outcome.

But we can't stop at the expense ratio when comparing the costs of various mutual funds. There are still four more cost categories we must consider.

1. Loads: Many mutual funds charge a 'load.' This is a sales commission assessed either at the front-end (upon purchase) or the back end (upon sale) of shares. At present, loads are limited to **a mere 8%** of the transaction amount.

Pundits leap to the conclusion that you should never buy a load fund when a no-load option is available. While often true, many load funds charge lower expense ratios which offset the cost of the load.

Remember, loads only happen once, but fees are extracted <u>every year</u>. It's very possible that a no-load fund with a higher expense ratio can be more expensive over a long period of ownership than a fund with a lower expense ratio that charges a load. Regardless:

Determining a fund's expense ratio: easy.

Determining a fund's load: relatively easy.

But the next three cost categories – are just as real as they are hidden and nearly impossible to determine. Yet they have a dramatic impact on your investing results.

2. Trading fees: Trading fees are embedded costs that the fund absorbs when it buys or sells securities held by the fund. The industry gets away with non-disclosure of these costs because they vary by the size of the transaction, and the volume of transactions from year to year.

But the fact remains that just like you and I, when a mutual fund buys or sells securities – it pays a transaction fee – on each end. And their transaction fees are not of the $7.95 variety that we can often access through discount brokers. They're often buying or selling hundreds of thousands of shares or bonds – where the transactions must be strategically and carefully layered or structured. The resulting costs can be significant.

One way to get some insight into transaction costs is to look at a fund's 'turnover' ratio. This is a measure of the proportion of the fund's assets that are bought and sold each year.

A fund with $1 billion in assets and a 50% turnover ratio, has $500 million in annual trading transactions – all of which trigger a transaction cost. If the turnover is 100% - its trading costs are based on $1 billion per year in transactions. Some funds have turnover rates in excess of 100% - and you can bet the trading costs in those funds are even more substantial.

A study by three academics, Roger Edelen, Richard Evans and Gregory Kadlec of the University of California, the University of Virginia and Virginia Tech, respectively, found that mutual fund trading fees cost investors **1.44% per year on average.** Whether the trading costs on your mutual funds are higher or lower – they go unreported because of their variability – but add cost nonetheless – meaning more of your money goes to pay for their trading whims – rather than into your retirement bucket.

3. Cash Drag: Another buried, and indeterminable cost inside a mutual fund is what's called the 'cash drag.' Nearly all funds maintain a portion of investor's (your) assets in cash. Why?

1. First, they need to be able to quickly redeem shares when investors move in and out of the fund. They must maintain cash reserves to do so.

2. Second, they typically invest in 'blocks' of securities and often need a large stash of cash on the sidelines to take advantage of a large block share purchase.

3. Third, funds hold cash when they liquidate one position and wait for the right market re-entry opportunity.

When money is on the sideline – not invested, it is earning nothing. If a fund maintains 10% of its assets in cash – 10% of your money is earning nothing – diluting the rate of growth on the fund's invested assets by the same 10%. That means, the cash drag alone can lower your return from 10% to 9% - and you'll never know it happened.

According to a study by William O'Rielly, CFA, and Michael Preisano, CFA, the average cost from cash drag on large cap stock mutual funds over a 10-year time horizon was **.83% per year**. Imagine – a cost that is nearly as much as the expense ratio – that is indeterminate and undisclosed!

4. Tax Drag: We're still not done. Another buried, and indeterminable cost of owning a mutual fund is its tax drag.

While the tax liability in your 401k may be deferred, the operator of the mutual fund doesn't have that luxury. When they make money on investments inside the fund, Uncle Sam comes knocking. When the fund pays their tax bill, where do they get the money? You guessed it – your holdings. It's reflected in the tax-adjusted price of your fund shares.

According to Morningstar, **the average mutual fund tax drag is 1.0% to 1.2% per year**. This means of course that one of those benefits of a 401k – tax deferral – which we've already proven to be a mathematical mirage – is untrue on another front. You ARE paying taxes while in deferral – in the form of the share price of mutual fund shares held in your account - which are paying their taxes as they go – out of your money.

Add it all up, and that harmless expense ratio your company or the company's third-party administrator says you're paying to own a fund is likely 2-3 times that amount. In fact:

Forbes believes the total cost of mutual fund ownership is between 3.17 and 4.17% - annually.

Think about that for a minute. The fund's manager must be so smart at picking stocks and bonds, that their expertise consistently beats the market by more than the total cost of fees and commissions before you'll ever net a dime's worth of profit from their expertise.

And while we're at it – if the fund must cover all its costs before the investor realizes a gain in their share price – who is getting paid first – and who is getting paid last?

That's right – once again – you put up all the money – you take all the risk – and you get paid last – assuming the fund does well enough to cover all its various costs first.

The sobering bottom line – **according to Standard & Poor's - is that over the last 15 years, 92.2% of large-cap funds lagged a simple S&P 500 index fund**. The percentages of mid-cap and small-cap funds lagging their benchmarks were even higher: **95.4% and 93.2%,** respectively.

Why? Not because fund managers are inept at picking stocks – but because you're paying so much more than you think in fees and commissions.

401k Owners Pay the Highest Rate of Fees & Commissions of nearly any account type

Surely this one can't be true – can it? It can, and here's how.

In Chapter 2, we learned that 401k owners are in a one-sided partnership with the government. We learned that you don't own all the money that appears on that 401k statement – Uncle Sam owns some of it. How much, we don't know – and won't know until we take it out.

But who's paying the fees and commissions on the entire balance in your account? That's right – you are - <u>which means you're paying the fees and commissions on Uncle Sam's money</u> – and you will continue to do so for the rest of your life (or at least as long as you leave your money in a tax-qualified account like a 401k or IRA).

Let's say future tax rates will be 30% on your account balance. You therefore own 70% of the money in your account – but you're paying the fees on 100% of that money.

Forbes says you're paying between 3.17% and 4.17% in fees and commissions each year. Let's use 3.5% as a sort of midpoint. When we divide 3.5% by 70% (the share of the account balance that's actually yours) – **we discover that you're paying a full 5% of your money each year in fees and costs.**

You're paying an annual 1.5% premium over and above what an investor in a non-qualified plan – invested in the same mutual fund is paying.

Your mutual fund must grow by 10% for you to realize 5%.

Now if your mutual fund breaks even, you lose 5%.

And if your mutual fund has a losing year? Well – you get the point.

Perhaps that explains why – month after month – year after year – your 401k never seems to perform quite as well as the market in the good months; and it always seems to lose a bit more than the market in the bad months.

In his later years, admonishing the very industry he helped invent, John Bogle, founder of the Vanguard family of mutual funds and widely regarded as the 'father' of the mutual fund industry said, *'the miracle of compounding growth is overwhelmed by the tyranny of compounding fees.'* A stark confession – and a truth moment - from a man whose genius has been hi-jacked by those who succeeded him.

Fees and commissions are eating you alive in your 401k or equivalent plan; and now you know a truth no one has ever told you before.

' I Want Money My Taxed at The Highest Rate Possible'

The lowest tax rate in the IRS code applies to capital gains. Capital gains taxes are assessed against investing gains where the underlying security was held for more than one year. Investments held less than one year are subject to 'ordinary income' tax rates – generally the highest rates in the Code.

Even though 401ks are usually held for more than one-year (often for several decades) they <u>never</u> benefit from (lower) capital gains tax treatment; and instead, are necessarily taxed at (higher) ordinary income tax rates - always.

As of this writing, taxpayers in the 10% or 15% income tax bracket pay a capital gains tax rate of ZERO. Those in all but the highest (39.6%) income tax bracket pay a capital gains tax rate of 15%. But instead of benefitting from a capital gains tax rate of zero or 15% - 401k owners will pay their ordinary income tax rate - 15% to 39.6% -

on the balance in their 401k in taxes — and that assumes tax rates in retirement are the same as they are today.

In other words, for many, ordinary income tax rates can be twice as much (or more) than would be assessed on long term gains were the same dollars in a non-tax-qualified account.

By simply deciding to build wealth through a 401k or similar plan, investors subject their money to the highest tax rates in the IRS code —.

All that bluster about pre-tax contributions and tax-deferred growth (which we now know to be a mathematical myth anyway) — is wiped out when money is withdrawn and taxed at higher ordinary income tax rates.

Translation: 401k owners take it in the shorts — again.

'I Want Limited Investing Options'

The range of investment options in 401ks is limited. The majority of choices are usually mutual funds. Some plans will offer a money market option; some will offer company stock; and others will offer variable annuities – but by far, mutual funds dominate the investing option landscape of 401k plans.

The choice of funds may cover a variety of investing objectives (income, growth, sector, international, yield, etc.), which provides a degree of flexibility, but few allow the purchase of individual stocks, bonds, or other securities that may offer the possibility of better returns and/or more safety of principal.

Want to invest in rental property or real estate? Sorry.

A friend's business? No such luck.

Antiques or collectibles? Not here.

Precious metals? Nope.

Why would we want to limit our investment options? We wouldn't shop at a grocery store that only offered 3 varieties of cereal – or cookies – or chips – or soda – or whatever. But we accept those limitations when it comes to our money?

Limited choices always mean limited outcomes – and that's the point. We should want to be nimble enough – and have a sufficient variety of investment options to capture every possible opportunity in front of us; and to avoid the pitfalls that might trap us or subject our money to unnecessary risk.

Qualified plans simply do not make the full spectrum of investing options available to those investing in non-qualified   plans.

'I Want My Income Tax Bill to Be as High as It Can Possibly Be'

There is one – and only one - guarantee with all qualified plans: <u>Your tax bill will be as high as it can possibly be</u>!

That's because 'compounding' applies not just to the growth of our money – but also to the growth of the deferred tax liability embedded in your account.

Consider a saver who starts saving $300 a month at age 27, and keeps it up until retiring at 67. Each month, our saver defers the taxes on those contributions. If we assume a 25% tax rate – they're deferring $75/month in taxes. Over the 40 years they contribute to the plan, they will have deferred a total of $36,000 in taxes.

Over that same time, the account would have grown to $787,444 at retirement (assuming a 6% growth rate). But the embedded tax liability at the same 25%), will be more than $197,000.

Deferring $36,000 so we can pay $197,000 doesn't sound like a very good deal. In fact, many would never have signed up if that outcome had been known to them up front.

Taxes are a problem. Why compound a problem?

Unfortunately, much of the 'learning' when it comes to the 401k, comes by way of hard lessons – many of which can't be reversed once the die is cast – the tax impact being one of them.

In historic terms, taxes are 'on sale' now! Since the advent of the income tax in 1913, most periods have seen higher tax rates than exist today. Given the financial condition of our country – many speculate that tax rates simply must rise again in the future.

So, if we're in a partnership with the government when it comes to qualified plans – and we recognize the nature of that partnership in a new way and want out – when is the best time to buy out a bad business partner?

When the buyout price is at its lowest. Is that now? Perhaps. Based on 100 years of tax rate patterns, history suggests that now might be the time.

' I Want to Lock My Money Up Until Retirement (Or Pay a Penalty to Get at It Before Then)'

Qualified plans like 401ks are designed to be retirement accounts only. That's why the IRS assesses a 10% penalty for us to access money before age 59-1/2 (with some very narrowly defined hardship exceptions).

The problem is that we usually look at savings – as savings. In other words, we don't usually make a distinction between 'retirement' savings – and ordinary 'rainy day' savings. And because we don't, we sometimes find ourselves needing access to our 401k (retirement) money - before retirement.

When that's the case, 401k owners will not only pay tax on the money they take out – but a 10% IRS penalty, too.

Qualified plan advocates urge us to pile all we can into these plans, conveniently leaving off the part about paying a penalty if we need to get at that money before retirement. And those needs seem to come at the most inconvenient of times – times where we have little choice other than to invade those 401k retirement savings.

Lose a job and need your money to see you through? <u>Penalty!</u>

Want to use your money to take advantage of a business opportunity? <u>Penalty!</u>

Here's what happens if you need $20,000 for.... whatever? Let's say your tax rate is 25%. Uncle Sam will demand his share the minute you take it out, and you'll be subject to a 10% penalty on top.

Divide $20,000 by 75% (to calculate the tax liability), then add 10% of the $20,000 you withdrew. You'll need to take out $28,666 to end up with $20,000 after tax and penalty for your need.

That means 35% of what you take out will have to be paid to Uncle. So – if you need $20,000 after his share, you'll have to withdraw $32,770 ($20,000 divided by 65%). That makes the true – effective tax rate on that withdrawal, a whopping 39%.

Imagine being charged 39% to access <u>your own money</u>!

Some plans offer the option of borrowing against your account balance as an alternative to taking a distribution and paying the tax and penalty. This is an even worse idea.

1. First, the money you borrow from your plan is not earning anything because it's not invested, inside the account. This imposes an opportunity cost which is just as real as a cash cost.

2. Second, you'll pay interest on the borrowed funds. The interest payments will come out of your already-taxed money – and go right back in to your 401k – where eventually, it will be taxed again when withdrawn. It's the ultimate in double-taxation.

3. Borrowed money must be repaid within 60 days of separation of employment. If a plan owner takes a new job or gets fired with an outstanding 401k loan balance, they'll have to come up with the cash to repay it in full within 60 days.

    Fail to do so and it will be treated as a 'distribution' – meaning it will be added to their income for the year – where it will be both taxed and penalized. What a deal!

Rainy days happen. Life happens. College happens. Opportunities happen. Why would anyone want to pay the government an additional fee to get at their own money – or alternatively, have to separate their savings into separate 'retirement' and 'non-retirement' buckets just to avoid the potential problems associated with 401k withdrawals or 401k loans?

'I Want My Family to Qualify for Less College Financial Aid'

All the so-called 'smart' stuff you're doing by saving for retirement in a 401k or other flavor of tax-qualified plan has another little surprise waiting for you when it comes time for the kids to go to college.

Every family with an interest in finding out whether they will qualify for need-based financial assistance from either the government or the college they choose to attend, will complete a FAFSA application.

FAFSA is the Free Application for Federal Student Aid. It is a lengthy, intimidating, financially invasive questionnaire that reveals your financial affairs – all of them – to the government, which then apply a formula of their own making - to determine whether or not you qualify for any help.

That formula is secretive, so applicants have no idea what answers on the FAFSA application will trigger what outcomes. But one thing we do know: unfortunately, FAFSA will <u>penalize applicants for the contributions they make to 401k and similar plans</u>.

That penalty will reduce, and could even completely disqualify them for need-based financial aid from either the government or the college.

The government theory is that if a family is putting $500/month in a 401k, they could just as easily pay a portion of that money for college instead. So, the family's qualification for need-based assistance is reduced based solely on their 401k contributions.

If you knew those contributions would reduce your eligibility, you would have two options:

1. Suspend your saving to maximize your qualification for assistance; or
2. Save outside a 401k plan during the college years.

No advisor would ever suggest suspending saving – so let's rule that one out. That leaves saving in an after-tax account of some kind. Woops! FAFSA catches you again with an even stiffer penalty for non-qualified assets (savings) that exceed another arbitrary, government-imposed, age-driven exemption threshold.

> As a sidebar, another 401k cousin designed specifically for college is the 529 plan. This is another form of one-sided partnership with the government – and it too is a trap, as 529 balances will also count against families completing the FAFSA application by lowering their eligibility for need-based college financial assistance. From a college financial planning perspective, 529 plans are among the absolute worst things families can put their money into.

It's hard to save for retirement – and even harder to save for college. That makes it seem a cruel injustice to penalize families for doing responsible things like saving through a 401k; or saving in after-tax plans – but in a way only the government can figure, both can reduce aid eligibility – which means college will cost more than it has to.

Later, you'll learn about a third option that will allow you to keep up your saving discipline without a FAFSA penalty – so you can maximize your qualification for need-based assistance.

For now, however, understand that among all the other foibles we've learned about the 401k already, these qualified plans can be college-financial-aid killers.

'I Want to Be Sure My Kids and Grandkids Don't Get All of What's Leftover When I Pass Away'

When we think about taxes at death – we typically think about the estate tax – and then quickly dismiss the subject because estate taxes are unlikely to impact us. *'Estate taxes only affect the rich people.'*

Sort of. While you may be safe from the estate tax, it's the income tax that is consequential when it comes to the balance in your 401k at the end of life. <u>What's left in our 401ks at the time of our passing is fully taxable to our heirs.</u>

There are two exceptions. We get one 'free pass' when our 401k or IRA passes to our spouse. The other exception is when we have a financial advisor who is smart enough to set up a 'stretch' IRA. Outside of those two possible escape clauses however, here's what will happen.

Upon death, the money left in a 401k or IRA account will pass according to your wishes (or your will/trust). Say there's $500,000 left when you pass away. You've arranged for each of your two kids to receive half. It's about then that your kids discover you had a third kid all along that they didn't know about. Congratulations – it's a boy – and his name is Uncle Sam.

Each of your two *natural* kids will have $250,000 added to the income they normally earn in the year of your death. The following April, they'll owe tax on the whole enchilada.

If your kids earn $50,000 each – and are in the 25% tax bracket, their 'take-home' pay would normally be $37,500. The year they receive their inheritance however, the IRS treats them as if they made $300,000 (their $50,000 of income, plus the $250,000 they inherit from you).

That could catapult them into – say – the 35% tax bracket. Their tax bill is suddenly swell to a whopping $105,000 (35% X $300,000), leaving them with just $195,000 each after taxes.

Since the normal tax on their own income would have been $12,500 ($50,000 – 25% in taxes), the tax burden on the inheritance is the difference between the $105,000 they'll owe – and the $12,500 they would otherwise owe on their own income. That difference - $92,500 – is the tax they'll pay on your inheritance - enough to make you roll over in your grave.

So, here's the bottom line.

- Kid 1 gets a $250,000 inheritance, less $92,500 in taxes, for a net of $157,500. That leaves them with 31.5% of your money.

- Kid 2 also gets a $250,000 inheritance, less $92,500 in taxes, for a net of $157,500. That leaves them too, with 31.5% of your money.

- Kid 3 (Uncle Sam) gets $185,000 – or 37.0% of your money.

<u>Uncle Sam will get more of your 401k leftovers than your own kids will!</u>

If you're fond of your children, that bit of news probably has you boiling mad. Chances are, you never intended for the 401k to be the *"I don't like my kids and grandkids all that much"* plan.

Even if you don't like your kids all that well – chances are the thought of Uncle getting more of your money than they will – is even more disgusting.

That $500,000 left over in your 401k is your life's financial legacy. Sharing 37% of it with the government probably wasn't what you had in mind – but that's exactly what will happen if you insist on dying with money left in your account.

'I Want My Money Constantly Exposed to Market Risk'

Based on our discussion of the limited investment choices offered by most 401k plans, the options we looked at were all market-based (except the money market) meaning they necessarily expose money to the risk of loss. Certainly, that includes just about any mutual fund.

The Wall Street Cartel would have us believe that we must assume some degree of risk if we expect to grow our money — or at least to grow it at a reasonable rate of return. But <u>risk is not a prerequisite for growth</u>, and nobody knows that better than the truly wealthy.

So how do the rich get richer — without exposing their money to market risk?

This story is from a friend who manages the money of the super-rich — and it confirms that those who are both smart and rich don't have to expose their money to risk of loss to make big gains.

Imagine you have $10,000,000 to invest. I know – that's a big number – but this is pretend – so let yourself dream a little!

You don't want to put a penny of your money at risk of loss – but you do want it to grow. So, you invest in a portfolio of bonds. Those bonds are safe, and carry a 5% coupon rate – meaning you can buy $10,000,000 worth of them for $9,500,000.   One year later, you'll be able to redeem your bonds for exactly $10,000,000.

Suddenly - you have $500,000 in your hand and a bond that is guaranteed to be worth $10,000,000 in a year – even if you flush the $500,000 down the drain. You've just immunized your whole $10,000,000 from loss.

You then use the $500,000 of cash (the bond's coupon) to invest in $500,000 of NewCo stock – a company you think is going to go up in value.

Fast forward one year – and one of three outcomes have happened:

1. NewCo ended up at the same price it started at. You sell your $500,000 of NewCo stock for the same $500,000 you paid for it. Added to your $10,000,000 in bonds, you have a tidy $500,000 profit for a gain of 5%.

2. NewCo went into the toilet and you lose your entire NewCo investment. You redeem your bond portfolio for $10,000,000 and break-even – having lost nothing.

3. NewCo stock grows in value by 20% - meaning your $500,000 investment is now worth $600,000.

You redeem your bonds for $10,000,000 and have a total of $10,600,000 for a 6% gain.

See how it works? No risk; and in two of the three scenarios you grew your money. In the third, you broke even.

In reality – Mr. Rich Guy would have purchased NewCo options and turned his $500,000 into several million had NewCo gained value - and he would have really made a killing. But options are a subject for another day.

If Einstein calls Compound Interest the 9th Wonder of the World – we probably ought to listen. But compounding cannot happen when we invest in things that have even the possibility of a loss associated with them.

Revisiting the Rule of 72 once again, we know that $1,000 will double to $2,000 in 10 years if we grow it at 7.2%. But what happens if we break that 10-year winning streak, and throw in one year with a little 5% loss?

Beginning Balance	7.2% Uninterrupted	7.2% with one year at -5%
	$1,000	$1,000
1	$1,072	$1,072
2	$1,149	$1,149
3	$1,232	$1,092
4	$1,321	$1,170
5	$1,416	$1,255

6	$1,518	$1,345
7	$1,627	$1,442
8	$1,744	$1,546
9	$1,870	$1,657
10	$2,000	$1,776

We don't end up with 5% less money at the end of 10 years - **we end up with 11.2% less** ($2,000/$1,776).

When is 5% equal to 11.2%? When it applies to our money and market losses! This is another example of John Bogle's 'tyranny of compound losses.'

That 'loss' may not look that significant, but it is. Back in chapter 5, we talked about a 27-year old saver putting $300/month away for the future. We said that if he grows his money at 7.2% for 40 years, he'll have $833,081 at retirement. Not a bad deal!

But what if our investor misses the growth mark by just 5%? Rather than growing his money at 7.2%, he grows it at 6.84%? His new retirement total is $752,937. Not only does he end up with $80,000 less. Think that will make a retirement lifestyle difference?

If the super-rich design strategies to avoid risk – shouldn't we – particularly with this new understanding of the cost risk can impose on our outcome?

As small and average investors, we simply cannot afford to be exposing our money to risk for our entire lifetimes. Yet we're forced to do so by the limited, market-based investment options made available to us in 401ks and other qualified plans.

Later – you're going to learn how to play the wealth-building game exactly like the rich guy did in the story we just looked at – and you'll be able to do it without all the fuss and muss of hedging bond and options.

'I Want My Retirement Lifestyle to Be Less Than It Can Be'

So far, we've looked at the 401k as an 'accumulation' vehicle – a way of building up a big fat account balance for retirement. You're probably beginning to question its effectiveness for doing that job.

But perhaps the 401k's greatest shortcoming reveals itself *at* retirement, when retirees quickly realize that it's not how much they have in their account – it's <u>how much income that account balance will produce</u>.

Income dictates lifestyle – and isn't lifestyle what retirement is supposed to be about?

While it may seem that the account balance and the income it will produce go hand-in-hand or are a function of one another *('the more I have, the more I can spend')* – it's not true.

The Wall Street advisory industry will typically suggest that their retiring clients draw between 2.5% and 4.0% of their account balance in annual retirement income. In their estimation, that gives the account owner a pretty good chance of not running out of money before they run out of life.

When it comes to running out of money, 'pretty good chance' is not good enough for most — but that too, is a topic for another day.

The real question is why such a low percentage? Even if we use the more generous end of the range and assume a retiree draws 4% out of their account annually for income — it's not far-fetched to think that the balance could grow at roughly the same 4% per year.

Take 4% out — and grow the remaining balance at 4% - and the retiree will draw down very little of their principal over their lifetime. In other words, they'll have roughly the same amount at death they started out with at retirement — <u>even if they never intended to leave a financial legacy!</u>

How can that make sense?

Leaving money to others is not a bad thing — and for many it is a high-priority financial goal — but the 2.8% - 4.0% rule doesn't even ask the question! If we assume the retiree's goal is to maximize retirement lifestyle rather than to leave a bunch of money to others — why would the Wall Streeter's promote such a modest income draw?

The answer to that question reveals both Wall Street's greed — and their inability to protect retirees against the new financial risks they take on in this phase of their lives.

First the greed part. If, by taking 2.8% - 4.0%, the retiree will die with about as much money as they retired with, then the Wall Street advisor never has to take a pay cut! Since they're charging fees and commissions on the account balance, they have a financial interest in the retiree spending less – so that account balance never goes down. It's a giant fee and commission ATM for them – that will last as long as you do! Their message to retirees: *"Sub-optimize your retirement lifestyle so I don't have to take a pay cut."* It's obscene in its audacity.

As if that weren't bad enough, the low income draw also reveals another gaping Wall Street shortcoming. In retirement, we take on a new set of financial risks – risks that didn't exist during the accumulation years. The Wall Street community is completely incapable of eliminating those risks. So, their default position is to let you 'hedge' those risks with your own money - in the form of an income draw rate that is artificially low. Those four risks:

- Market risk (the risk of loss of principal)

- Tax-Rate risk (the risk of higher future tax rates)

- Health-event risk (the risk that a retiree could need access to a lump sum of money for a health-related event), and

- Longevity risk (the risk of outliving one's money)

Consider how the Wall Street '4% rule' deals with these risks:

1. If the market goes south in mid-retirement, the 4% income drawdown rule permits the account owner to continue their income at the same level even if the principal sustains something akin to the 40% market crash experienced in 2008-2009.

2. Likewise, if tax rates skyrocket in retirement, the 4% figure has enough 'margin' to absorb a

greater future tax burden without forcing reduced retirement income.

3. Maintaining a moderate income draw also preserves enough principal to hedge against the risk of the account owner needing access to a lump sum for a catastrophic health event or a long-term-care need.

4. The more modest draw provides a hedge against the account owner out-living their life expectancy and running out of money for income.

The Wall Street message is, "Live with less income than you could have – because we here in Wall Street-land need to keep getting paid - and are completely incapable of eliminating the four financial risks inherent in retirement.'

The solution you'll read about shortly eliminates all four of those financial risks – allowing retirees far more retirement income on the same account balance. Hear that. The alternative you're about to meet will produce far more income – safely – than a 401k or other qualified plan will – even if the principal balance in the account is the same!

It is borderline criminal that Americans are forced to resign themselves to sub-optimizing income – and in return a sub-optimized retirement lifestyle - for the simple reason that it is not in the economic interest of an entrenched community of Wall Street advisors to steer their clients to a better alternative (because they don't have   one).

' I Want to Pay Taxes on Money I May Not Need'

Some will achieve financial success outside of the 401k. Perhaps they'll sell a business, or inherit money, win the lottery, or experience some other kind of financial windfall over their lifetime. Maybe they have the benefit of participating in one of the few remaining traditional pension plans.

Their good fortune may put them in a position where they don't need to draw from their 401k for retirement needs. They have other sources of money to support them in retirement. Perhaps they'd just as soon give it away or leave it to their family or heirs – anything other than take it out for the sole purpose of paying taxes on it.

But when they reach age 70-½, along comes Uncle Sam who declares that he's done waiting to collect his portion of the partnership – and he wants his money - now! He calls it Required Minimum Distributions – or RMDs –

and it's little more than <u>forced taxation</u> of money that may not be needed to support lifestyle.

Based on a formula of his choosing – which – as the only partner with a vote – he can change at any time – retirees are forced to take money out of their 401ks for the sole purpose of having it added to their income and taxed.

Often, this can throw the retiree into a higher tax bracket – which means they keep less of the income they already had – like Social Security income.

RMD's may not seem like a big deal – but paying tax on money is no fun. Paying taxes on money that's not needed for retirement lifestyle is even less fun.

Yet the one-sided nature of the partnership means that both the time limit for the deferral of taxes on a 401k balance (currently age 70-½), and the minimum distribution requirement (currently about 4% per year at age 70-½), are both subject to unilateral change.

As you read the next two chapters, keep in mind that RMD's alone can be the trigger that causes Social Security benefits to be taxed – and Medicare premiums to increase.

In other words – RMD's are a big deal.

' I Want My Social Security Check to Be Taxed'

Ask 100 people if Social Security benefits are taxable and the majority will say 'no.' The majority would be wrong. At least some portion of most recipients' Social Security benefits will be taxed.

Oh well – at least it's just 'rich' people who have their benefits taxed, right? Uh – wrong again. Unless of course you consider those earning more than $25,000 (including ½ of their Social Security income) to be rich.

To determine what portion of your social security benefits will be taxed, you must first calculate your MAGI – or Modified Adjusted Gross Income.

MAGI starts with AGI – or Adjusted Gross Income from the 1040 tax return; and ADDS back non-taxable interest income, plus one-half of your Social Security Benefit.

Confused yet? Perhaps that's on purpose. It's not the formula that's important – it's the result the formula imposes that is.

Based on MAGI, the following table will determine what portion of Social Security benefit must be added to income and taxed at the recipient's corresponding rate:

Income – Single Filers	Maximum Taxed Portion of Social Security	Income – Married Filers
$0 - $24,999	0%	$0 -
$25,000 - $33,999	50%	$32,000 -$43,999
$34,000 +	85%	$44,000 +

So, a single filer drawing as little as $25,000 a year in retirement income (including half of their Social Security benefit) can have up to 50% of their Social Security benefit taxed!

A couple earning more than $44,000 per year (also including ½ of both recipients' combined Social Security benefits) will have 85% of their benefit taxed.

When you think about it, Social Security is really the return of taxes that have been confiscated from our income throughout our entire working lives. It doesn't seem quite fair that money that was first confiscated as tax - under force of law – could be taxed again when it is returned to us in the form of Social Security benefits later in life.

Take a couple who is entitled to a total of $35,000 in Social Security benefits. If they live 20 years in retirement, that's $700,000 in benefits they would collect if they weren't taxed. But if 85% of their benefit was taxed at 25% - they would pay $150,000 of that benefit back to the government.

That's a $150,000 additional tax they didn't tell you about when you signed up for the 401k – and adds more evidence to the argument that you may NOT in fact be in a lower tax bracket in retirement – even if your income is less.

What may be even more concerning however is how the Social Security Administration is going to deal with the reality of less money coming in from taxes; and more money going out in benefits, as our population ages.

<u>Given the choice of government reducing benefits, or tweaking the brackets in the table above, which do you think is more politically likely</u>?

The point is – there is likely more to come – so the motivation to immunize your Social Security benefits from taxation now, should be a financial priority.

Unfortunately, relying on retirement income from plans like 401ks and others leaves your Social Security benefits squarely in the cross-hairs of a government whose appetite for tax revenue is insatiable.

What the government giveth (pre-tax contributions and tax-deferred growth) – the government taketh away (taxation of Social Security benefits).

'I Want to Pay Higher Medicare Premiums'

Medicare is essentially health insurance for the retired. It may not be something you're thinking about now – but if you enjoy employer-provided or other good healthcare coverage today – you're going to want to continue receiving good healthcare coverage when you're retired – and Medicare is it.

Provided by the government, Medicare is an 'entitlement' all may take advantage of. Historically, Medicare has been funded through taxation of your income. In fact, 2.9% of your lifetime income tax has gone to fund Medicare.

But in recent years (much like Social Security), the 2.9% 'tax' has not been sufficient to cover the expenses of the program. Additionally, more benefits have been added to the program – most recently – prescription drug coverage.

Medicare has four 'parts.'

- **Part A** – covers hospitalization expenses and is generally available without an additional premium

- **Part B** – covers the cost of doctor visits, tests, therapies and other related expenses not involving hospitalization or non-emergency-related drugs.

- **Part C** – is offered by private insurers, and fills in the coverage gaps left between Parts A, B, and (usually D). There are many alternative plans to choose from, and premiums vary accordingly.

- **Part D** – covers prescription drugs, and is an optional add-on to the other Medicare parts.

The majority of Americans (those who worked a W-2 job for at least 40 quarters over their life), pay no premium for Part A, but will pay a premium for any Part C coverage they may choose.

Parts A and B are mandatory for Social Security recipients (certain narrow exceptions apply), and the premium for Part B coverage is deducted directly from your Social Security check.

Premiums for Parts B and D (part D, while voluntary, it is elected by most retirees because it covers prescription medications) are 'means-tested' – meaning the premiums you pay are based on your income.

What is your income?

MAGI – the same formula used to determine the taxability of your social security benefits as discussed in the previous chapter. And the higher your income – the higher your means-tested Medicare Premiums will be.

In other words, that 401k income we've been talking about, can cause you to pay <u>higher Medicare Premiums for Parts B and D coverage</u>.

This is the next chapter in the story of, "as the government giveth – the government taketh away." Only this time, it's even more open-ended.

The difference between the Part B and D premium for a couple – from the lowest possible premium to the highest, is a whopping **<u>$8,000 a year – and it's on the rise annually</u>**.

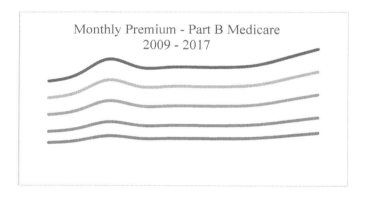

This chart shows the trend in Part B premiums over the last several years in each 'income band' from low to high. The Part D premium evolution reveals a similar trend.

There are two important takeaways from this chart you need to know about. First, without increasing direct taxes or otherwise taking on a difficult political position, the government has a handy (and well used) mechanism through which it can claw away more of your money each year through these premium adjustments – and its called 'means-testing.'

While the current income brackets are frozen until 2019, the premiums are not. We can expect nearly continuous premium increases – and in 2019 estimates suggest that a large segment 'middle-class' retirees who currently escape means-testing will become subject to it – and can expect higher Medicare premiums as a result.

The second observation is the widening gap between the increases imposed on the lower income bands – and those applied to the higher income bands.

Much more of the increases are born by those with higher incomes. And remember – a primary source of 'countable' income is going to your 401k or other qualified plans.

Medicare means-testing – just like Social Security means-testing, is a silent tax no one talks about. But it is real – and once you're retired – these taxes are inescapable.

What's worse, as you learn about the alternative we'll reveal later, these taxes are completely voluntary – because we're going to show you a way to immunize both your Social Security benefits – and your Medicare premiums from taxation and means-testing – forever - no matter how much 'income' you   might draw from the plan in retirement.

'I Don't Want a Premium-Free Long-Term Care Benefit.'

While those of you in the millennial and younger crowd may be tempted to ignore all this stuff about taxes, Medicare, Social Security, and Long-Term Care – those who are there already will tell you they wish they'd paid more attention at your age – while there was still time to do something about it.

The reality is that thanks to diagnostic and medical technology, we're living longer. That means the younger you are, the more important is the information you're about to learn.

<u>There is a 75% chance that you will need long-term-care of some description – in your lifetime.</u>

Stand in a circle with your three closest friends, and only one of you will get out of here without some sort of nursing home or assisted living need at a 'today' cost of about $80,000 a year – a figure that is growing at an alarming rate.

Obviously, 401ks and other qualified plans provide no 'benefit' for that eventuality, leaving you with only one choice (other than crossing your fingers) — and that is to buy long-term-care insurance. But that option too is riddled with problems and challenges of its own. Traditional Long-Term Care Insurance — the kind your parents had:

1. Is almost extinct. Few insurance companies even offer long-term-care coverage — so getting it can be hard, if not impossible.

2. Long-term-care premiums - like car insurance premiums, are a 'use-it-or-lose-it' proposition. If you turn out to be the one-in-four that never needs the benefit, you'll have nothing to show for the lifetime premiums you paid.

3. Most of us delay purchase long-term-care coverage until our later years when the premiums are at their highest — often prohibitively so.

4. Benefits are typically 'reimbursement' benefits, meaning the insured must both incur — and pay for the expense first - then submit a claim for reimbursement from the insurance company.

5. Benefits must be used for 'qualifying' expenses — meaning the insurance company gets to say what they'll cover and what they won't.

6. Premiums will not be tax deductible or tax-free for most taxpayers.

Long-term care is a financial landmine for retirees — and one that is more likely than ever to become a real issue for more people. Combined with fewer options to deal with the risk, and the rate of inflation related to medical and long-term care costs, this is among the most underestimated of all financial risks to retirees.

Living Benefits

Medical technology, diagnosis, and treatment is constantly increasing our life expectancy. In fact, life expectancy has increased nearly 10 years since just 1970.

More than a quarter of today's baby boys, and a full one-third of baby girls will live to age 100. But 7 out of every 10 Americans will require long-term care.

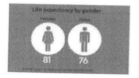

It's a near statistical certainty that one spouse in a married couple will require long-term care.

More daunting, the 'cost' of long-term care now exceeds $80,000 nationally, far more in some markets

When you get to the 'solution' section of this book, you'll discover a plan that not only blows away the 401k on most all fronts, but it offers a built-in long-term-care type benefit that overcomes <u>all</u> the shortcomings of traditional long-term-care coverage.

'I Want to Limit the Amount of Wealth I Can Accumulate'

n the eyes of the government, too much of a 'good thing' is – well - a bad thing. That's why the government limits the amount of money we can contribute to plans like the 401k.

This chart is not comprehensive, but does cover the current limits that apply to most plans.

Plan Type	Contribution Limit
401k, 403b, 457	$18,000
SIMPLE	$12,500
IRA	$5,500

While there are certain 'catch up' provisions that apply to plan participants who are over 50, the chart shows the contribution limits imposed by the government for those who wish to take advantage of the pre-tax contribution features of the plan. Additional contributions can often be made – but they will not be tax-deductible.

Non-deductible contributions create the potential (if not the likelihood) of a second problem. Unless certain forms are filed both when the non-deductible contributions are made – and when withdrawals are taken (likely decades down the road) after they're long forgotten, taxed contributions may also be taxed as distributions – another example of double-taxation.

The real point of the discussion is that plan participants are limited on the amount they can save – which means they are effectively limited on the amount they can accumulate – and in turn – are limited by the amount of available income in retirement – which translates to retirement lifestyle.

These limitations make it very difficult to rely on these plans as the primary portion of our retirement income.

And remember – with private pensions on the way out, and Social Security on shaky ground – 401ks and other qualified plans have become the centerpiece of many Americans' retirement. Contribution limits only exacerbate a problem that is already plagued with peril.

Consider this. The average American will earn $2,000,000 over their lifetime. The Social Security tax that will be imposed on that income will be 15.3% - a far greater rate of savings than most Americans will contribute to their 401ks.

Yet – the average Social Security benefit is only $16,322 as of this writing. So, if a 15.3% 'saving rate" generates only $16,322 of retirement benefit – how much extra is it reasonable to expect the 401k will add to that figure when there are such strict contribution limits?

It may be a pretty safe bet that we'll invest our 401k money more wisely than the government will invest what they take from us in the form of Social Security taxes – but if we contribute 6.2% to our 401ks – which is half the rate Social Security taxes out of our paychecks (they take 12.4% currently) - we'll have to <u>double our investment performance just to supplement our Social Security income with another $16,322</u> from our 401k.

And oh, by the way – <u>we can run out of money in our 401k</u> – while Social Security will (presumably) pay us no matter how long we live.

'Everything in moderation' should not apply to saving money. We should save as much as we possibly can. Contribution limits constrain the production of wealth, limit retirements and inheritances, and give American workers a false sense of security regarding their retirement prospects.

Part 2

The Alternative

CHAPTER 17

What A Better Plan Looks Like

Y ou're about to discover what I – and thousands of other financial professionals – consider to be a far superior alternative, and one that is available to almost all Americans.

First, I want you to see how this alternative overcomes every single one of the 16 negatives about 401ks and other qualified plans that we've covered so far.

As we dive in, I want to suggest a framework – an 'ideal' model we can use to evaluate this alternative. I call this ideal model the **Ultimate Wealth-Building Blueprint**.

The Ultimate Wealth-Building Blueprint has two components – a set of outcomes we *don't* want – and a set of outcomes we *do* want.

What we Don't Want

Given the choice, all of us – without exception – would want to save our money in a way that protects it from the *Three Wealth Killers*: Market Risk, Taxes, and Fees & Commissions.

Your 401k – as well as most securities, investments, vehicles, and accounts you might use to save money and build wealth, suffer from all of the **Three Wealth Killers**.

Think of your 401k as a bucket of money. But your bucket has three holes in it – labeled: <u>Market Risk</u>, <u>Taxes</u>, and <u>Fees & Commissions</u>. Money is constantly escaping your bucket through those three holes.

Sometimes they're pinholes and the leakage is relatively benign. At other times, they're gaping gushers with money pouring out in large quantities at frightening rates.

- Money leaks out of our bucket when market losses take money out of our bucket – and put it in someone else's – never to be ours again.

- Money leaks out of our bucket when it is taxed – whether taxed 'today' or 'tomorrow,' and

- Money leaks out of our bucket when fees, commissions, and other investing costs are taken out of our account by our brokerage houses, advisors, employers, and others.

The impact of the Three Wealth Killers cannot be overestimated or overstated.

Let me introduce you to what I call your 'Zero Gravity Number.' Your zero-gravity number is the figure money can grow up to be if it is immune from market risk, taxes, and fees. We use the zero-gravity number to demonstrate the impact of the Three Wealth Killers.

Consider this example:

A 35-year old saver who puts $500/month into a savings plan, and grows it at 7.2% for 30 years will accumulate $681,662 by the time he reaches age 65.

At a 4% annual income draw, that saver would enjoy retirement income of $27,266 — relatively assured for the rest of their life.

But what happens when we impose a bit of the Three Wealth Killers on their money?

- What if we take 1.5% per year out of their account for fees and commissions?

- What if we interrupt the 30-year string of 7.2% gains by introducing one year that is down 5%, one that is flat, and one that is down 10%?

- What if we apply a 25% rate of taxes on the retirement balance and retirement income?

Get ready:

Outcome	Zero-Gravity Number	With the Three Wealth Killers
Balance at Retirement	$681,662	$427,084

Income in Retirement	$27,266	$17,083 = (45%)
'Cost' - Financial Gravity	$-0-	($254,578)=(37%)

The Three Wealth Killers – applied in what even my critics would agree is a very modest (if not ridiculously low) quantity – results in 37% less money – and in turn 45% less income in retirement.

By the way – once our investor reaches retirement, the meter continues to run – meaning that throughout their retirement years – and yes – even death – the Three Wealth Killers will continue to extract more of the investor's money in a constant outflow from their bucket.

Our goal must be to protect our money from leakage of all kinds!

What We Want

What we do want, is for our money to benefit from the *Five Money Needs*: Safety, Growth, Income, Liquidity, and Tax-Efficiency.

- Safety – we don't want to be in a position where we can lose money again - not a penny – ever!

- Growth – we want to capture the power of compound interest so we know we'll always have more money tomorrow than we have today.

- Income – we want to know that at some point in our lives, we can turn our money into an income stream – hopefully one we can't outlive.

- <u>Liquidity</u> – we want to be sure we can get to our money when WE want – and to do so without a government-imposed penalty.

- <u>Tax-Efficiency</u> – we want to accomplish all this in with the smallest possible tax impact.

Look at them once again. Think 'ideal' here.

Is there anything you aspire for your money that's not on the list?

Is there anything on the list of money needs that is unimportant to you or your money - or that you would take off the list?

If you could invest your money in a way that immunized it from the Three Wealth Killers and ensured that it benefitted from the Five Money Needs – all of them - at the same time – without tradeoff – would you be in a better financial position than you are today?

That's why I want you to evaluate the alternative I'm about to reveal, against the <u>Ultimate Wealth Building Blueprint</u>.

To get there, we have to look at combining two separate strategies – or buckets. Neither of the buckets will get us to that ideal destination on their own – but the combination of – and interaction between the two - will deliver you as close to the Ultimate Wealth Building Blueprint as we can possibly get.

CHAPTER 18

Bucket One

Bucket one is what we call a <u>Money Contract</u>. While that may be a new term to you, chances are you'll recognize it as we unpack how it works.

A bank CD – or certificate of deposit - is a form of money contract. CDs differ from typical investments in that the purchaser is buying a <u>future value that is guaranteed by contract</u>. They're not making an investment whose outcome is based on the chance performance of a security or market.

Money contract earnings come from contractually guaranteed interest that is credited to the pledged principal amount. In exchange, the buyer agrees to leave their money locked in the CD for a contractually defined period of time, and will usually have to pay a 'penalty' to access their money before the certificate's maturity date.

Maturity dates can vary from a few months – to several years; and the interest rate usually is higher the longer the 'lock-up' commitment.

CDs are most often purchased by seniors who don't want to expose their money to market risk, and appreciate the near absolute safety of banks. But CDs have one major drawback – they're boring! They typically pay anemic interest rates and are therefore lousy vehicles for accumulating wealth or generating retirement income. Most CDs will not even grow at a rate where the invested principal keeps up with the rate of inflation – meaning they're actually going backward in terms of purchasing power.

The 'opposite' of a CD, is the stock market – where returns can be spectacular – but <u>nothing</u> is guaranteed. In fact, stock market investors (you're one of them if you own Mutual Funds) can lose 100% of their money at any time.

While investors like the <u>safety</u> aspects of bank CDs – the growth potential is anything but exciting. Stock market investors on the other hand, love the <u>growth potential</u>, but the risk exposure scares the heck out of most people.

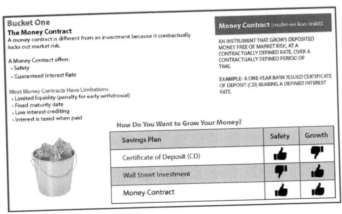

Bucket One
The Money Contract
A money contract is different from an investment because it contractually locks out market risk.

A Money Contract offers:
· Safety
· Guaranteed Interest Rate

Most Money Contracts Have Limitations
· Limited liquidity (penalty for early withdrawal)
· Fixed maturity date
· Low interest crediting
· Interest is taxed when paid

Money Contract (muhn-ee kon-trakt):

AN INSTRUMENT THAT GROWS DEPOSITED MONEY FREE OF MARKET RISK, AT A CONTRACTUALLY DEFINED RATE, OVER A CONTRACTUALLY DEFINED PERIOD OF TIME.

EXAMPLE: A ONE-YEAR BANK ISSUED CERTIFICATE OF DEPOSIT (CD) BEARING A DEFINED INTEREST RATE.

How Do You Want to Grow Your Money?

Savings Plan	Safety	Growth
Certificate of Deposit (CD)	👍	👎
Wall Street Investment	👎	👍
Money Contract	👍	👍

The money contract you're about to meet offers the <u>safety</u> features of a bank CD – with the <u>upside growth potential</u> of the stock market, which makes it a very exciting alternative.

It accomplishes this by crediting interest to the principal through a strategy called <u>Equity Indexing</u>.

An example of an 'equity index' is the Dow Jones – or the S&P 500, or any of several others. Earnings credited to this kind of money contract are based on the gain or loss of a particular index over a defined period of time – most commonly - one year.

> *But if an index can go down – as they sometimes do - how is money protected from the potential of a loss?*

The investor's money is never invested **in** the index, rather interest is credited based on the performance of the index. How that is accomplished involves a discussion of bond yields and stock market options. While beyond the scope of our discussion here, the detailed answer to how this is accomplished is actually quite brilliant – and surprisingly interesting.

Additional protection comes in the form of a contractually guaranteed 'floor' rate also guaranteed by contract. The floor is usually zero percent – but can be as high as 2.5%, sometimes even more. Floor rates protect both the money contract principal as well as locked in gains – and are guaranteed for the life of the contract.

In exchange for this downside protection, this kind of money contract also has a limit on the upside potential. The most common limitation is an earnings 'cap.' When index performance exceeds the cap, the money contract credits the cap rate, but no more. There are other ways money contracts calculate earnings credits:

- Some credit interest based on the performance of the index monthly rather than annually.

- Some may not have a cap – but instead have a 'spread,' where the contract issuer subtracts a fixed portion of the upside gain, and credits the rest.

- Still others use a 'participation rate,' where the contract owner gets a percentage of the index movement over the measurement period.

The table below shows how money contracts work based on various scenarios.

Interest Crediting Method			
S&P Index	Annual Point to Point – 0% Floor, 13% Cap	Annual Point to Point – 80% Participation Rate, no Cap	Annual Point to Point with a 2% Spread, No Cap
If the index goes up by 15%	Contract earns cap rate of 13%	Contract earns 80% of 15% = 12%	Contract earns 15% - 2% Spread = 13%
If the index goes up by 7%	Contract Earns 7%	Contract Earns 80% of 7% = 4.9%	Contract Earns 7% - 2% = 5%
If the index goes down by 15%	Contract Earns 0%	Contract Earns 0%	Contract Earns 0%

Equity-Indexed money contracts typically have another set of common characteristics.

- They offer 'fixed interest rate' crediting options just like a CD, although the fixed rate is often <u>several times the interest rate paid on a typical bank CD</u>. It's not unusual for money contracts to pay a fixed rate of 3-4% when CDs are at 1% or less — and there is no 'lock-up' period with a money contract.

* Like a bank CD, there is a penalty if you want access to <u>all</u> the invested principal. However - you can usually get to <u>the majority</u> of the principal without a penalty.

* From an 'institutional safety' point of view, the kind of Money Contracts we're talking about are issued by insurance companies - which protect investors as well - arguably better, than banks.

But that's about where the similarities end — and where the kind of money contract we're talking about begins to really get interesting.

First, when interest is credited to a money contract, it is not taxed until it's taken out — so it preserves its tax-deferred status as long as it remains in the contract.

That's a huge advantage. A bank will send you a 1099 for the interest earned on a CD the minute the interest is credited — and that creates an immediate tax liability.

The other advantage of our kind of money contract — and this can't be overstated — is that <u>when earnings are credited to the contract they become part of the principal balance and are immediately and permanently protected from any possibility of future loss</u>.

This *'lock and reset'* feature eliminates the necessity for market-timing (guessing when to take profits or re-enter the market). Once earnings are credited they can never be lost.

In order for Einstein's Ninth Wonder of the World (Compound Interest) to work, there cannot be the possibility of loss. When money contracts lock out the risk of loss and lock in gains through the 'lock and reset' feature, we leverage the power of uninterrupted compounding, distinguishing a money contract from just about any other alternative, anywhere.

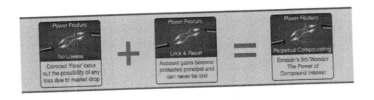

Let's take a look at the power of this equity indexing concept. What you see on the chart below is a comparison of what would have happened over the 15 years from 2000 through 2015 in the market.

- The <u>lower line</u> is the actual S&P 500 index performance over that time.

- The <u>upper line</u> shows how an equity-indexed money contract with a 0% floor and a 13% cap would have performed in the exact same index, over the exact same period of time.

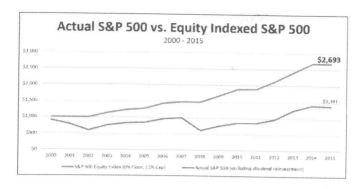

Not only would the Equity Indexed Money Contract have produced nearly double the amount of money as the market itself, but an equity indexed money contract with a floor and cap would outperform the market itself over almost any 15-year period we might choose to compare.

That's because it turns out that it is <u>much more critical to lock out losses than it is to capture the full gain in those years when the market's performance exceeds the cap rate.</u> We absolutely see that at play in this example.

Look at 2000, 2001, and 2002 on the chart. All were down years in the market – yet we see the floor rate (0%) protecting the balance of the Money Contract balance so it doesn't participate in the market's losses.

We see the same thing happen again in 2007 and 2008 – when the market goes down but the Money Contract doesn't. In fact, look how long it takes the lower line to climb back to $1,000 (its 2007 pre-crash starting point) - a full 5 years.

Let's summarize what we've learned about equity indexed money contracts.

- We can choose to grow our money using an equity-index which gives us the downside protection of the floor rate – and the upside potential of the cap rate,

- We can choose to have a fixed rate of interest credited to our money that is typically several multiples of what banks offer,

- We can blend the two – putting part of the money in the fixed rate account, and part in the equity indexed account to create our own custom 'floor' while still benefitting from upside potential,

- And we can change our mind from time to time as allowed by the contract – sometimes even daily!

With this understanding of the features and mechanics of a money contract, let's review which of our <u>Wealth Building Blueprint</u> objectives we're able to check off before moving on:

- We've eliminated market risk – one of the Three Wealth Killers

- We've assured that our money will benefit from the Money Need of 'Safety'

There are several objectives yet to go, but we're off to a pretty good start.

CHAPTER **19**

Bucket Two

To check off more of our objectives, we need to introduce the second bucket — a life insurance account.

There Is More Work to Do

The Second Bucket - Life Insurance Bucket

What does Life Insurance have to do with <u>wealth building</u> or <u>retirement income</u>?

Let's Talk About Life Insurance

Things We Like About Life Insurance
- Life Insurance inexpensively secures your financial future - even if you cannot complete the job
- Life Insurance provides a death benefit that passes to your heirs tax-free

Things We Dislike About Life Insurance
- We have to pay those pesky premiums to keep the policy going
- The death benefit goes to others and we have no ability to use it while we are living

Let's flip the traditional view of Life Insurance on its head:
Life Insurance builds a 'bucket' of money that is passed to your family upon your death. This money comes to your heirs tax-free and can be built to a significant size over your lifetime.

What If...
- You could get access to the death benefit while you are still alive?
- This access was available without regard to your age or stage of life?
- Access was available for qualifying medical and long-term care needs?

Now two reactions probably leap to mind immediately.

1. I don't really like the stuff, and

2. What in the world does life insurance have to do with building wealth and retirement income?

Both are completely legitimate reactions, and the answers reveal why we use a life insurance bucket — so let's get to it.

First, everyone knows they need life insurance — and not a group plan through an employer that goes away if we leave the job — but insurance that we own and control.

Life insurance is the only way we can know that the job of securing our family's future will be completed even if we're not here to do it ourselves. We don't have to like it — but we do have to have some.

What else do we <u>dislike</u> about life insurance?

1. We don't like paying premiums, and

2. We don't particularly like the idea that others will get all the benefit after we're gone!

I get it.

<u>But what if we turned the whole idea of life insurance completely upside down? What if we looked at life insurance through a whole new 'lens?'</u>

What if we could…

- Access the insurance account value (death benefit) during our lifetime rather than only at death?

- Get at that insurance account money regardless of our circumstances or stage in life?

- Take money out tax-free and penalty free - at any time?

- <u>Base our retirement income on the (larger) life insurance account balance rather than the (smaller) money contract balance – and have much more retirement income as a result</u>?

- Access even more of the life insurance account value if needed for qualifying medical or long-term-care needs?

<u>There is a very special class of life insurance that does all these things</u> – and as a result, it lets us check off most of the remaining boxes on our Wealth Building Blueprint.

This information is huge – but it's likely to be foreign to whatever understanding of life insurance you may have held until now – so let's unpack what we have just covered.

Accessing the Death Benefit while we're still living

To understand how this is possible, we first need to understand that the issuer of the money contract we've been talking about, is the same insurance company that offers the life insurance benefit. In fact, both accounts - or 'buckets' are bolted together into one power-packed product called <u>Indexed Universal Life Insurance, or (IUL)</u>.

Because both buckets are part of the same product, the money contract bucket serves as (secondary) 'collateral,' allowing the life insurance bucket to act as a 'line of credit' that we can draw from at any time – for any purpose.

That's how we're able to keep our money in the money contract, *and* access portions of the insurance account at the same time.

The combination of a money contract and an insurance account represented by Indexed Universal Life Insurance, means our money can essentially do two jobs simultaneously.

- It is our *savings balance* – growing and compounding with all the features and flexibility of the money contract we just covered; while

- The life insurance bucket can serve as a *spending balance* – including serving as a great source of reliable retirement income.

What's more, we can use the life insurance account for life needs like major purchases, college, marriage, or as an emergency or opportunity fund.

Access money regardless of our circumstances

With the money contract serving as a perpetual (and growing) source of collateral, we can access portions of the life insurance account without any fanfare.

We don't have to apply – we don't have to prove income or assets – we don't have to be working – we don't have to be healthy - and it doesn't matter how old we are or what stage of life we're in.

This 'on-demand' access feature allows us to simply call up the insurance company (or complete an online form), tell them how much we want, and where to send or deposit the money – no questions asked.

Access money tax-free and penalty-free

And the hits keep on coming!

Thanks to IRS Code Section 7702 – perhaps the last, greatest tax advantage in the entire tax code for ordinary people, we can draw that money out <u>tax-free and without penalty</u>.

It is Code Section 7702 that permits all life insurance death benefits to pass income tax free. That same provision gives us tax-free access to money in the life insurance account (the death benefit) during our lifetime.

And because the life insurance account is not 'qualified' like the 401k, there are no penalties for early access. There are some special limitations – and these life insurance contracts must be carefully designed by an expert - but this is a fabulous feature.

Base retirement income on the insurance benefit

Upon request, the insurance company will calculate a withdraw amount (think: retirement income) that we can draw down forever (or at least until age 100) without ever running the account out of money.

The amount we can take will be based on the (larger) insurance account rather than the (smaller) money contract account. Therefore, <u>this strategy will almost always produce significantly more income than any competing Wall Street account – including a 401k</u> – with a similar balance.

This can be a little difficult to follow, but we'll demonstrate by way of an example a bit later. It's worth noting that by taking income from the Life Insurance account, we <u>never touch the Money Contract balance</u>. That means two things.

- First, the money contract benefits from uninterrupted compounding - forever, and

- Since the Money Contract bucket and the life insurance bucket are bolted together — our friend, IRS Code Section 7702 allows the Money Contract balance to be added to the insurance benefit at death — and <u>the whole thing passes on to our heirs - tax-free</u>.

Access more money for a long-term-care need

While the insurance company will put some limitations on the amount that can be drawn out of the death benefit for ordinary needs or retirement income, there are different (and higher) limits for certain long-term-care needs.

Should the policy owner need additional money or income for a qualifying health event, there is a provision in the contract for that.

Not only does this permit a higher income draw while healthy (because there is no need to hold cash in reserve for such an event), but there is usually no premium cost for this benefit until/unless it is needed.

<u>Think of it as 'premium-free' long-term care coverage</u> — something the 401k (or anything else for that matter) could never contemplate. It's like car insurance that you don't have to buy unless you wreck the car — wouldn't that be nice?

Many Americans in the 50+ age range are using this kind of insurance account primarily for this reason alone since traditional long-term care has become so expensive and inaccessible.

CHAPTER 20

The Fine Print

Now when we use the word 'advance' to describe the income draws we're able to take from the life insurance account — you may be thinking, *'that sounds a lot like a loan.'*

You're right - it is.

We're actually borrowing against the policy's death benefit. And when we hear the word 'borrow' we naturally think of interest rates and payments. But this is where the insurance company does us another series of significant favors:

- First, the interest rate charged on advances is usually quite low (mid-single-digits), and owners usually have the option of either a fixed or variable rate. What's more, most contracts 'cap' the lifetime interest rate at a very modest maximum.

- The insurance company will 'capitalize' the interest — meaning they add interest charges to the loan balance. Owners can repay the balance if they choose, but can also choose to <u>never</u> repay the loan. Those taking advances during their working years usually choose to repay them since doing so will boost the availability of retirement draws — but those taking advances as their retirement income typically choose not to repay the loan, allowing the death benefit to do so later on.

- If we elect not to repay the advances, the insurance company guarantees that the loan balance — including all the interest that accrues over a lifetime — will be repaid from the death benefit itself. We never have to worry about finding another way to pay the loan balance.

  This will reduce the death benefit accordingly, but most people are much more interested in maximum retirement income than they are the death benefit in their later years. Besides, most people's need for pure 'death benefit' coverage subsides as they get older anyway — making this a great vehicle.

The bottom line is that the insurance account serves as…

- The source of advances,
- The source of the interest owed on advances,
- The primary source of collateral for advances, and
- The source of repayment of those advances — including all the accrued interest

And it's all guaranteed by contract!

What's more, accessing money couldn't be easier:

- There are no qualifications,

- There are no income requirements,

- There are no employment, age, or health requirements,

- No application or other documentation is required,

- There are no restrictions on what the money can be used for,

- There is no tax on advances taken out,

- There is no penalty on advances we take out,

- And no assets or other outside collateral is required. The policy itself backs up all the advances.

The contract limits how much of the insurance account can be accessed, but the limitations are generous, permitting access to most of the money contract balance on demand, and generating more retirement income than a similar balance in any other kind of account would likely permit.

While the interest rate almost doesn't matter (since the insurance company guarantees that the death benefit will be sufficient to repay it), there is another way to look at policy loan interest that makes it even easier to wrap our heads around.

Since advances against the insurance account are available tax-free (thanks to IRS code section 7702), the interest charge could be viewed as the 'price' policy-owners pay in exchange for tax-free access.

It doesn't take a rocket scientist to conclude that a 5%+/- interest rate on policy advances is far cheaper than the combined federal, state, and local income tax that would otherwise be assessed on the same amount taken out of just about any other kind of account, including the 401k.

What's more, if we look as the interest expense as a tradeoff against paying taxes – the 'tax' (interest) is 'deferred' in the sense that it doesn't have to be paid until death – at which point it will simply be deducted from the death benefit.

In fact – since the death benefit is likely to far exceed the premiums paid in – one could even argue that even the interest that is owed to the insurance company after a lifetime of tax-free retirement draws – is paid by the insurance company, too – via the death benefit!

CHAPTER 21

To Borrow – or to Withdraw?

So why take 'advances' against the insurance account if they trigger interest charges - rather than just withdrawing money from the money contract account where there is no interest charge?

Good question – here's the answer.

First, by never touching the cash in the money contract, it continues to grow and compound, while the tax liability continues to be deferred. If we take that money out for another purpose – it cannot grow for us.

> *'But doesn't deferral mean we'll someday have to pay taxes on that money – just like a 401k?'*

No. If we take money we need from the insurance account rather than the money contract account, our good old friend IRS Code Section 7702 presents us with another very special feature. At death, <u>the accumulated money contract balance will be added to the life insurance account, where it will be passed-on income-tax free</u>!

Think about the power of that for a moment. Can you imagine a better deal? Money that would otherwise be taxed – can be converted into fully income-tax-free money?

Now sometimes, that raises another question, "What if I want to get at the cash in my money contract?"

The good news is that you absolutely can. Just like a bank – you can go to the insurance company and demand your money at any time – no questions asked. Here's what you need to know about doing so however:

1. For the first several years of the contract, there is a 'surrender' charge that limits the amount of your money you can withdraw without paying a surrender charge – or partial surrender charge.

    Surrender charges vary from contract to contract, and usually apply for 10 years +/-. No surrender charge is applied for withdrawals that fall below the surrender charge threshold.

    Surrender charges are typically in the 10% – 15% range, and go down each year. But if we treat these as long-term plans – typically for retirement (which we should), we only want to put long-term money into them. Stick to that strategy and the surrender penalty is a non-issue because as the plan ages, the surrender charge fades all the way to zero.

2. Second, if we take out more than what we've put in – we're taking out 'gains' rather than 'principal' –we'll have to pay taxes on those gains.

    Since one of our goals is to never pay taxes again, it's almost always better to take money from the insurance account (where all we'll pay is the low, loan interest rate) rather than the money contract account (where we would pay income tax on the gains).

3. Finally, if we take money out of the Money Contract account, it cannot grow and compound. When we leave it in – it can. If we want all the benefits of compounding – we're much better off taking advances against the life insurance account than the money contract account.

All that said however, we can absolutely withdraw money from the money contract at any time – its just wise to know the both the implications and the available options.

CHAPTER 22

Parlez-Vous Francais?

L et's look at another opportunity built into this arrangement that can be very powerful. It's called Arbitrage – a fancy French word that describes the relatively simple concept of the difference between two interest rates.

Arbitrage may sound a bit scary – or sophisticated (, it is sophisticated, but not scary – so once you've learned this – try it out at your next party – people will be really impressed)! Let's look at it by way of example:

	Money Contract Balance	Life Insurance Account Balance
Amount Needed	$100,000	$100,000
Interest Rate	+ 7%	-5%
Outcome	+$7,000	-($5,000)

Assume for a moment you need to get at $100,000 for a need of some kind. Both your money contract and your insurance account balances are sufficient that you could take the $100,000 from either account.

Let's also assume that the <u>return</u> credited to your money contract is 7%; and the <u>interest rate</u> charged on advances from the insurance account is 5%.

- If you withdraw $100,000 from the money contract account, you will <u>not</u> earn the 7% interest. That's called a 'lost opportunity cost' – you lose the opportunity to make $7,000 – and it's very real.

- If you borrow from the policy, your account would be <u>charged</u> 5% interest, or $5,000.

Arbitrage happens when you do both at the same time. By not touching the money contract value, it grows by $7,000. By borrowing instead from the insurance account, you'll incur an interest charge of $5,000. In other words, <u>you just got paid $2,000 to access the $100,000 you needed</u>.

- The transaction didn't cost you $7,000 in lost earnings as it would have had you taken a withdrawal from the money contract,

- The transaction didn't cost you $5,000 in interest as it would have had you simply borrowed the money at 5% from an outside source.

- The transaction took advantage of both, netting you a $2,000 gain – all because of the interaction of the two buckets of money inside an Indexed Universal Life Insurance policy.

That's arbitrage – the difference between two interest rates – one earned; and one paid.

Having both a money contract and a life insurance account with virtually unrestricted access to cash gives us the opportunity for positive arbitrage.

Before we leave the subject of arbitrage however, we need to acknowledge that sometimes arbitrage can be <u>negative</u>.

In the example above, if the money contract had earned the 'floor' rate of zero (or for that matter, and interest rate less than 5%), the borrowing cost would have been the $5,000 charged on the policy advance, with no (or only partial) earnings in the money contract to offset it.

A good advisor will find you a money contract with the best earning potential – and a life insurance account with a lowest policy loan interest rate so that your potential for <u>positive</u> arbitrage is maximized, and your risk of <u>negative</u> arbitrage is minimized.

If you don't like the idea of arbitrage at all – positive or negative - (and many don't), most plans can be structured to exclude the possibility altogether so there's never a concern. What's more – this arbitrage lockout option can usually be turned on or off at will – providing the policy-owner flexibility regarding their appetite for arbitrage.

CHAPTER 23

Whadda Ya Want for That Thing?

’m guessing you’re wondering what this kind of feature-rich combo-platter is going to cost – right? That’s not only a fair question – it is a question you need to get in the habit of asking no matter what you do with your money now that you better understand the impact of fees, commissions, and other investing costs.

Let me give you the bad news first. We can’t avoid fees altogether. That’s probably not a surprise. But there’s a ton more good news that far outweighs the bad. In fact, the fee structure in an Indexed Universal Life insurance policy is one of its primary advantages. Here’s how:

1. There is a fee that is charged on the money you put into the money contract. This only applies when you put money in – and in most contracts, it’s only charged for the first 10 years. You are never charged on your future earnings or the deferred tax portion as you would be in a Wall Street account. While it tends to ‘front-end-load’ some of the cost – it also represents a huge

reduction in the overall lifetime cost structure of the plan.

2. Second, the 'mortality' charges (the cost of the pure life insurance benefit), is inexpensive and ensures that your family will be financially protected in the event of your premature death.

    However, it's also worth noting that the internal mortality charges look like a bell curve when charted – meaning they start low – grow – then recede again in the later years. This is a far different cost pattern than applies to anything in the Wall Street World where the cost curve continues upward – unchecked - as the account value grows.

    In fact, Wall Street exacts their fees even in years where the account owner loses money. That cannot happen in an IUL contract since losses are locked out.

3. Third, a professional advisor will be able to show you a projection of the total lifetime costs for your plan. Neither your employer nor anyone in the Wall Street world could – or would – give you that kind of information. Unlike Wall Street's game of fee obfuscation and fee opacity, these plans come with complete fee transparency – always an advantage.

4. Fourth, a professional advisor will construct your plan so that it results in the lowest fees possible. They'll do that by depressing the life insurance account (always being sure your need for life

insurance is met) to the lowest level allowed by the IRS. Since the life insurance account is a primary driver of the plan's expense, proper construction will not only lower overall plan costs – it will also ensure that the largest part of your deposited dollar goes into the money contract account.

5. Fifth - would it be fair to say you have no idea what you're paying in the plan you're in now? If that's true, then it is also impossible to know what you're getting for the money you are paying. In this kind of plan however, you can know not only exactly what you're paying – but exactly what you're getting for your money.

    a. A tax-free Life Insurance benefit,

    b. Tax-free access to retirement income,

    c. Penalty-Free access to money whenever you want it,

    d. Uninterrupted Compounding,

    e. The Elimination of market risk on 100% of your money,

6. Sixth, the fee structure in this plan works in the exact opposite way it does in a typical 401k or Wall Street plan. With 401k plans, fees are tied to the account balance. As the balance grows, the fees grow along with it.

In this kind of plan, fees start out higher, but diminish – sometimes all the way to zero in the later years.

<u>Almost any IUL plan – constructed as we've suggested – and held for 20 years or more – will result in a far lower lifetime cost than just about any competing plan – anywhere.</u>

The chart below demonstrates this by comparing the ending cash balance of accounts with various fee structures ranging from no fees (a baseline) – up to 3% in fees (less than what experts think we pay over a lifetime). Included is the money contract balance in a sample Indexed Universal Life plan such as we're describing.

As you can see – the IUL yields a considerably higher account balance after 30 years than an account with even 1% in fees and commissions. In fact, it comes impressively close to the zero-fee line.

7. Seventh, many money contracts offer a 'persistency bonus' - additional interest that is credited to the money contract account. Persistency bonuses usually apply when the plan remains in force beyond 10 years.

Think of it as a 'loyalty' reward. This bonus interest is paid by the insurance company, over and above the equity indexed crediting rate the plan owner would normally earn. The persistency bonus will often completely offset (or more), the entire cost structure of the plan.

Persistency bonuses vary from contract to contract, and can reach up to 1% of additional interest credits each year.

In the chart
of the reaso
converging

In fact, if the chart were projected out
another 20 years, the lines would actually
cross, and the IUL would be less expensive
than a competing plan with no fees or
commissions at all earning the same rate of
growth!

8. Finally, our plan does something no Wall Street
    plan could contemplate – and a Wall Street
    Advisor would scoff at, if proposed. It essentially

refunds your lifetime fees through the tax-free death benefit. Try asking your employer or Wall Street advisor if – after charging you a lifetime of fees – they'd do you the favor of refunding all those lifetime fees back to your estate when you're gone.

You can probably imagine the reaction.

The bottom line is this – while we can't avoid the fee impact altogether – we can minimize its impact during our lifetime, and neutralize it when we're gone.

Does that sound like a fair arrangement?

Does it sound like a better path than you may be on right now?

CHAPTER 24

Check, Please

W e're in the home stretch – so let's check our scorecard and see how we're progressing against the goal set we started out with when we introduced the idea of the Ultimate Wealth-Building Blueprint.

We got the party started with the money contract which checked off three important boxes for us.

Defeating the Three Wealth Killers

1. With either fixed-rate interest crediting or the option of equity indexed earnings with a zero percent earnings floor, Indexed Universal Life locks out any possibility of loss from market **risk**.

2. IRS Code Section 7702 means we lock out income **taxes** when we take money out through policy advances. Additionally, we immunize our money from future income tax-rate-increases of any kind.

3. While we can't escape **fees** altogether, we can ensure that 1) they are low, 2) that we know exactly what we get for the fees we pay – and that 3) they're essentially refunded through the life insurance death benefit.

Ensuring the Five Money Needs

1. Being a contract rather than an investment, we achieve **Safety** – one of our Five Money Needs. We can take even more comfort knowing that money contracts are issued by insurance companies – among the oldest, and most financially stable institutions in existence.

2. Because the value of our money contract account can only be flat (at worst) or up, we're assured of **growth** – one of the Five Money Needs.

3. The insurance account also positions us to not only generate income – but to generate more

income per dollar of cash than any competing account we've ever researched.

4.   We have two measures of **liquidity** – another of our Five Money Needs. First, our money contract balance is accessible on-demand. Second, the insurance account also provides us with liquidity through its 'line-of-credit' feature.

5.   The money in our money contract account grows tax-deferred, and will be added to the tax-free death benefit. Withdrawals up to 'basis' are tax-free, and advances against the insurance account are also tax-free (and penalty free). The resulting **tax-efficiency** of tax-deferred growth, tax-free access, an income-tax-free legacy, and exemption from all future taxes and tax increases is simply unbeatable. You can't get more tax-efficient than zero tax.

Adding it All Up

The Three Wealth Killers

- **Market Risk** – eliminated by adding a Floor and Cap
- **Taxes** – eliminated by using tax-free 'advances' from the insurance account
- **Fees & Commissions** – neutralized by the benefits of the life insurance contract

The Five Money Needs

- **Safety** – achieved by 'floor' protection and the 'lock & reset' feature
- **Growth** – achieved by eliminating the possibility of loss
- **Income** – achieved by the insurance account 'advance' feature

- **Liquidity** – achieved by application-free, penalty-free, anytime access to money
- **Tax-Efficiency** – achieved by IRS code section 7702

If the Ultimate Wealth Building Blueprint represents a set of criteria for evaluating investment options that is consistent with what you aspire for your money – this step-by-step analysis should lead you to the conclusion that IUL checks off all the boxes – and in a way no other alternative we're aware of – can.

CHAPTER 25

Revisiting the Not-So-Sweet 16

We're Not Quite Done Yet

While we may have vanquished all Three Wealth Killers; and assured ourselves access to all Five Money Needs – at the same time – and without trading one for another, we also want to go back and look at the 16 chapter titles we covered in Part 1 of this book.

1. **'I want to be deceived by mathematical trickery'**

   In our chapter on mathematical trickery, we talked about the fact that there was no mathematical advantage to pre-tax contributions and tax-deferred growth <u>when</u> there is an option to build wealth with after-tax dollars – grow those dollars tax-deferred – and then access those dollars tax-free. That's exactly what an Indexed Universal Life insurance policy does.

   Critics might argue that the interest which accrues on policy loans (the most efficient way to access money tax-free) is the equivalent of a tax. I would disagree for the simple reason that the insurance benefit is guaranteed to extinguish not only the interest on the loans – but the loan principal too.

In other words, the dollars that will pay any accrued interest comes from the same insurance company – not the owner's cash. It's almost as if they're charging interest – then paying the bill themselves.

Even if we concede the point that interest charges are a cost that is born by the policy-owner to escape taxation, the reality is that we should be thrilled to pay an interest rate on policy advances of 4% -6% to escape a 20% - 40% in income taxes – or more!

2. I Want to be in a One-Sided Partnership'

The bad news: an indexed universal life insurance policy is also a one-sided partnership, but this time you're the partner that is in sole control of everything related to the policy.

With a 401k, the investor puts up all the money – the investor takes all the risk – yet Uncle Sam has the sole right to decide what portion of the investor's money will become his when it's taken out. The investor has no voice in the matter.

All life insurance policies on the other hand, are considered 'unilateral' contracts. This is a legal term meaning that the only party bound by law to perform is the insurance company. The policy-owner has no contractual obligation whatsoever – and that's a powerful distinction.

Not only is the unilateral nature of life insurance a great benefit, but the word 'contract' also has special meaning. Unlike the open-ended relationship 401k owners have with Uncle Sam, their employer, and the stock market, every element of the insurance arrangement is defined and locked down by contract. <u>You know</u> <u>everything the insurance company **can, must,**</u> <u>and **can't** do</u>. You are in control – 100% - and it's all in writing.

3. **'I want to pay the highest fees and commissions possible'**

We learned earlier that 401k fees are higher than just about any other kind of account or investment going. This is a result of the high fee structure of mutual funds combined with the fact that 401k plan owners pay fees on Uncle Sam's money their entire lives. We also noted that indexed universal life has seven key 'cost' advantages over any other kind of Wall Street account, including the 401k:

1) Fees are assessed on deposits – not on the account's (growing) balance,

2) Lifetime fees are disclosed and projected upfront,

3) Policies are structured for lowest possible fee impact,

4) You know exactly what you get for the fees you pay,

5) IUL has a declining fee structure versus a 401k's increasing fee structure,

6) The persistency bonus often offsets fees as the policy ages,

7) Lifetime fees are essentially refunded via the death benefit

To cap it off – most owners of indexed universal life policies will pay substantially less in lifetime fees than they would in a competing 401k or other Wall Street account.

4. I want to give up the opportunity to have my money taxed at the lowest rate possible'

Forget ordinary income tax rates – capital gains tax rates, alternative minimum tax – or any other kind of income tax. Indexed universal life provides the option of tax-free today, tomorrow, and forever.

5. 'I want to limit my investing options'

Being forced to select from among a limited number of investing options, all of which involve risk, means it is significantly harder for a 401k plan owner to capture market opportunities and avoid market slides.

With an Indexed Universal Life policy, not only is risk locked out by definition, but policy owners have the ultimate in diversification by having interest credited to their money contract based on the performance of the entire market index – <u>without ever being directly invested in the market.</u>

Truth be told - diversification is a made-up Wall Street term. It has validity <u>only in the presence of risk</u>. Take away the risk – and diversification is utterly unnecessary.

6. 'I want my income tax bill to be as high as it can possibly be'

<u>401k:</u> Highest tax bill possible

<u>IUL:</u> Tax-deferred growth, tax-free access, income tax-free legacy.

Nuff said!

7. 'I want to lock my money up until retirement – or pay a penalty to get at it'

With certain rare exceptions, the money in a 401k is not accessible until age 59-½ without a 10% penalty - on top of the taxes owed on withdrawals. By comparison, the money available in an indexed universal life insurance policy is accessible on demand, tax-free, and penalty-free via policy advances or withdrawal of 'basis.'

8. 'I want my family to qualify for less college financial aid'

While 401k contributions negatively impact a family's qualification for need-based college financial aid – 100% of the money in your money contract *and* 100% of the money in your insurance account, *and* 100% of the money you save through money contract deposits - are <u>exempt</u> from the calculation that determines aid eligibility. This can make a major difference in the net cost of college for many families.

9. 'I want to be sure my kids and grandkids don't get all of what's leftover when I pass away'

Because 401k/IRA funds have never been taxed, they will be fully taxed when passed on (unless certain alternative arrangements are made); and they will be taxed at the recipient's ordinary income tax rate in the tax year of death.

In an indexed universal life policy however, the money contract balance is added to – and becomes part of – the death benefit. That benefit passes on income tax-free. The only tax possibility is that of estate taxes – and then only if the total estate value exceeds the exemption threshold.

If an estate is taxed, the heirs will be doubly glad life insurance was part of the plan – as the insurance company's death benefit is likely to cover most, if not all, of that tax.

10. 'I want my money constantly exposed to market risk'

With the option of the money contract's fixed rate - or the 'floor-protected' indexed crediting rate, market risk is taken completely off the table.

Next time the market nosedives (as will inevitably happen a few times over one's lifetime), and neighbors and co-workers are in a panic — you'll be sipping an umbrella drink by the pool — completely unaffected and unconcerned by the market's schizophrenia.

11. 'I want my retirement lifestyle to be less than it can be'

You may recall that those who retire with a 401k, IRA, or similar qualified plan will likely be advised to limit their income draw to 4% or less of their account value annually. This pathetically low rate is driven by the need for a Wall Street advisor to hedge against three retirement risks: the risk of <u>market loss</u>, the risk of <u>higher tax rates</u>, and the risk of a <u>catastrophic health event</u>.

Indexed Universal Life insurance negates the first two, and provides an additional, premium-free benefit in the event of the third. The result is an income draw rate that will often be **<u>10% or more</u>** of the money contract account balance — meaning far more retirement income than any competing plan could possibly contemplate.

12. 'I want to pay taxes on money I may not need'

Qualified plans like the 401k, have forced taxation on money that may not be needed through Required Minimum Distributions. IUL has no RMD requirement (not that it would matter since money can be taken out tax-free anyway).

13. 'I want my Social Security check to be taxed'

Social Security benefits are taxed in part, when income from sources that include the 401k, exceed very modest thresholds established by the IRS. This can have the effect of lowering the recipient's net Social Security benefit – or effectively increasing the retiree's effective tax rate substantially.

Income taken from an indexed universal life policy however – whether taken as advances against the death benefit, or withdrawals of basis from the money contract, are exempt from the equation that determines the taxability of Social Security benefits.

If all – or even a majority of your retirement income is derived from your IUL, you may never have your Social Security benefits taxed.

14. 'I want to pay higher Medicare Premiums'

The same applies to means-tested Medicare premiums. Income taken from an IUL is exempt from the formula that determines means-tested Medicare premiums. This IUL advantage is even more significant because there seems to be no limit to how high the government will raise Medicare premiums for this important – and partially mandatory program.

15. I don't want any kind of premium-free long-term-care benefit.'

The 'living benefits' in an IUL come with the plan, and are premium-free. They provide additional access to the insurance account value for qualifying events – that – in most policies, include Critical, Chronic (like cognitive impairment/Alzheimer's), Terminal illness – and in some cases - critical accident benefits.

Qualifications for receiving the benefit are similar to those of traditional long-term-care insurance – typically the inability to perform 2 of the 6 ADLs (Activities of Daily Living).

If the benefit is ever accessed, the portion of the death benefit that is 'accelerated' is discounted – the only real 'cost' of the benefit – which arguably is not a cost at all – rather the recognition of a pre-life-expectancy distribution of a portion of the death benefit.

This feature carries even more value in that rather than a <u>reimbursement</u> benefit (like traditional long-term-care insurance), an IUL's accelerated living benefit is almost always an 'indemnity' benefit. That means three things.

- First, it is typically available tax-free.

- Second, it can be used for anything – including to compensate family members or friends for their assistance; travel, alternative, non-covered or experimental treatments, therapies, etc.

- Third, it can be accessed <u>before</u> an expense is incurred – rather than after, and via a claim process as is the case with traditional long-term care insurance.

16. 'I want to limit the amount of money I can accumulate'

The IUL plans we've detailed do not have statutory contribution limits like 401ks and other qualified plans. As a result, there is no limit on contributions, accumulation, income, or legacy value.

Only the insurance company can impose a limit – and theirs will be based on each individual's 'insurance capacity' – a much more 'subjective' and generous figure.

But Wait – there's More

There are two other important features of indexed universal life insurance that we want to look at before moving on.

- All the money in these plans is protected from creditors and from probate – so the asset protection features of IUL are enormous.

  This benefit can be particularly appealing to business owners and entrepreneurs who must be extra vigilant about protecting their personal assets from an attack that may spill over from a business-related event.

- IUL can help you qualify for a mortgage and/or get the best rate available. How? By using the advance feature to temporarily pay off other debts prior to applying for a mortgage, your debt-to-income ratio will be lower – either qualifying you for a mortgage you might not otherwise have gotten – or qualifying you for a lower interest rate.

  Mortgage providers don't consider loans from an insurance policy as debt. Why? Because – as we've said previously – they don't have to be repaid.

Summary

Every one of the 16 'catches' we associated with the 401k are negated by indexed universal life insurance. So, in addition to achieving our goal set of eliminating the Three Wealth Killers; ensuring that our money benefits from the Five Money Needs, we can now add 'overcoming the 16 other drawbacks and limitations of the 401k.'

The evidence is overwhelming – the case is closed!

CHAPTER 26

Yeah, but...

'This sounds too good to be true' - 'why haven't I ever heard about this before' – 'there must be hidden risks!'

Have any of those thoughts crossed your mind yet?

Well – as I said earlier - you haven't heard about it because such a small percentage of the financial industry promotes it. Mainstream advisors hide it because of the threat it poses to their sweet little market-centric, risk-based, diversification-driven, fee-generating monopoly.

Much of the rest of the industry hasn't been properly trained or qualified in the products and strategies we've talked about. Even the insurance companies that offer these plans require additional, rigorous training that many advisors simply avoid.

Despite this, American families are finding professional advisors who are informing them of their options, and are constructing custom-crafted solutions based on their clients' needs, which is moving thousands into IUL-based alternatives every day.

As for 'too good to be true' – no plan is without risks – and that includes indexed universal life insurance. Let's look at the risks so you can arrive at a fully informed opinion.

Surrender Charges

During the first several years of the policy (usually 10 – 15 years), not all the cash that's in the money contract is available for withdrawal. That's because the insurance company is recouping some of its upfront costs for marketing, selling, underwriting, and supporting the policy. Should an owner request more money than is available – or should they cancel the policy, the insurance company will withhold a percentage of the money contract value as a penalty for early access/termination. This is called a 'surrender charge.'

Surrender charges are actually beneficial to policy-owners in two ways.

1. The surrender charge is only a 'potential' charge. Most owners who start these plans for the long-term will never encounter a surrender fee as it fades away to zero over the surrender period as defined in the contract.

2. The insurance company uses the surrender charge to recover its upfront costs over time as an alternative to recovering those costs all upfront in a lump sum. If they took all their fees up front, the owner would have less cash working in the Money Contract. Therefore, surrender charges are a benefit to the owner compared to the alternatives.

Deferred Tax Liability

The money contract is funded with after-tax dollars – and grows on a tax-deferred basis similar to a 401k. If a policy owner withdraws more cash than they put in (their basis), there will be a tax liability. Withdrawals up to the cost basis are not taxable, and of course money taken out in the form of advances against the insurance benefit is not taxed at all.

So, while a cautionary consequence to be aware of, most people will never knowingly or willingly take money out in such a way – or in such a quantity so as to ever trigger a tax event. Nonetheless – in the interest of disclosure, we want to highlight it here.

Negative Arbitrage

We defined arbitrage (that fancy French word) as the difference between two interest rates – and talked about the reality that in order to have the opportunity of benefitting from positive arbitrage we must assume the possibility of negative arbitrage.

Negative arbitrage can be a real issue if it happens for several years in a row. Thankfully, there are stopgap options built into the contract to negate the impact of negative arbitrage.

On some very rare occasions, negative arbitrage can mean an owner has to reduce the amount of income they're drawing out of their plan; and in even more rare circumstances an owner could need to put more money into the policy to keep it from collapsing and triggering a tax liability.

The chances of that are so remote as to be negligible, and would require both the policy-owner and the advisor to be completely asleep at the wheel, but again, in the interest of full disclosure, it's worth a mention.

Moving Caps

You'll recall that our money contract comes with an earnings floor and an earning cap. Floor rates are almost always locked in for the life of the contract, but the contract likely will provide the insurance company the option of moving the cap rate at its discretion.

Of course, caps can move **up** just as easily as they can move **down**. There is always pressure on the insurance company to keep caps at the highest possible level – and raise them when they can. This competitive pressure makes them slow to lower caps, and quicker to raise them – but again – disclosure requires us to acknowledge the possibility.

Internal Policy Costs

Next is the 'risk' of the insurance company increasing its internal policy charges. While most insurance contracts do allow the insurance company to change the internal cost structure, the number one cost component is the cost of the life insurance account (death benefit).

A good advisor will construct a client's policy in a way that minimizes the insurance benefit (and therefore the internal cost) to the lowest level allowed by the IRS (while being sure the client is adequately insured).

The reality is that these 'mortality' costs are generally going <u>down</u> - not up – a trend that has prevailed for more than a century, as medical diagnosis and treatment continues to expand life expectancies. While a risk – it is one that is far more likely to work in our favor than *against* us.

The IRS

There is a risk that the government – in particular – the IRS, could change code section 7702 and those changes could impact the tax-free nature of these plans. In fact, it has already happened three times in history – so we have some clue as to what the likely consequences might be if they take a fourth swipe at these plans.

Each of the previous three modifications impacted only new plan owners. Existing owners were left alone – or 'grandfathered' in. For some, that could be motivation to 'get in while the gettin's good.'

Institutional Failure

The last risk is probably the most obvious one – the long-term viability of the insurance company backing up the plan.

A good advisor will work only with companies that are highly rated by the major rating agencies that track insurance carriers: Standard & Poor's, Moody's, A.M. Best, and Fitch.

These rating services publish their findings – so a bit of internet research can provide ample information about a given company's financial viability and long-term prospects.

Most insurance companies offering these kinds of plans have been in business well over 100 years, meaning they've survived every financial calamity the world has thrown at them – including the Great Depression, the Polio epidemic, stock market crashes, world wars, you name it. In fact, far more banks failed in the Great Depression than insurance companies.

Insurance companies are probably the safest, most conservatively managed financial institutions on the planet – which explains their longevity and survival rate.

Additional reserve requirements, state guaranty funds, and other mechanisms are in place to ensure the safety of policy-holder contract values.

1) The Insurance Carrier could go out of business
- There are three levels of safety net to avoid this concern
  - Use only the best carriers
  - Carrier reserve requirements
  - State Guaranty funds

2) Earnings 'Cap' could decrease
- Driven by interest rates and options costs (volatility)
- Infrequent, small, and more upside than downside

3) Increases in Policy Charges
- Primary driver is mortality charges which rarely go up

4) Surrender charges for early termination or early access to money
- IUL is designed as a long term account only
- No cost when account is maintained past the surrender period

5) Tax liability on Surrender or lapse of policy
- This policy should be considered a lifetime investment
- Completely avoidable when policy is used properly

6) Possibility of 'Negative Arbitrage'
- Only a risk when income is turned on
- Can be completely locked out if desired
- Necessary to experience 'Positive Arbitrage'
- Flexible - can be turned on and off at owner's discretion

7) Future changes in Tax Law
- Has happened three (3) times in the past
- All existing owners should be 'grandfathered' in at contract terms

Are there risks? Of course. Everything in life has risk. The goal is not to avoid risk altogether – but rather to understand risk, understand what levers are at your disposal to manage risk – and to leverage the rewards, while avoiding 'paralysis by risk analysis.'

CHAPTER 27

The Case of Jack and Jill

Consider two retirees – Jack and Jill. They worked hard all their lives for the same company and saved dutifully. Both saved $500 a month for 37 years – from age 30 until now, when they're both 67 and retiring.

Jack put $500 in the company's 401k plan where their generous employer matched his contributions by 50% – adding another $250 every month. Jill on the other hand, allocated her $500 a month to an indexed universal life insurance policy. However, since her $500 had to be taxed first, she was only able to put $350 per month into her plan after taxes – with no company match.

By all appearances, Jack had made the much better decision. At $750/month (his $500 plus the company's $250 match), he was putting away more than twice as much as Jill's $350/month.

Jack and Jill both grew their money at 6.5% over those 37 years. After fees (1.5% of Jack's annual account balance), Jack ended up with the tidy sum of $960,376 at retirement. Hallelujah – Jack was nearly a millionaire!

Handicapped by her lower after-tax saving rate, Jill had just $551,901 in her money contract – although her insurance account had $763,439. The insurance account balance gave Jill some hope since she knew this figure would drive her retirement income.

Jack's financial advisor told him he could draw between 2.5% and 4% from his account each year in retirement income. If Jack wanted to be more certain that he'd never run out of money he'd stick to the low end of that range.

But Jack felt reasonably comfortable, and planned to take the maximum of 4% - or $38,415 each year as his income in retirement. Of course, he'd have to pay taxes on that amount – which – at the same 30% Jill had paid on her contributions, would leave him with just $26,890 each year to live on.

Jack questioned the 30% tax rate assumption because he'd always been led to believe he'd be in a lower tax bracket in retirement. But he was reminded by his tax advisor that because of increased tax rates and fewer tax deductions (kids, mortgage interest, and others) than he had earlier in life, his tax rate would be roughly the same 30% it had been in his peak earning years.

Jill's insurance company on the other hand, informed Jill that she could take $54,336 in advances from her indexed universal life policy with the even greater certainty she wouldn't run out of money. Because Jill's IUL income would be tax-free, she would enjoy just shy of twice as much as Jack would retire on. Jack and Jill were both shocked at the disparity between their two income figures.

After consulting with their respective advisors however, they learned that Jack's income draw was limited so that he could maintain his standard of living if tax rates went up – or if the market took a nosedive – or if Jack needed to get at money in the event of a long-term care need.

But Jill's plan had locked out tax rate risk – along with market risk from the minute she began to fund her plan. And with an additional built-in long-term care benefit, Jill didn't need to worry about that possibility either. As a result, Jill was able to comfortably draw considerably more income each year, than Jack.

Considering how diligently he'd saved – and how wise he'd been about his investments - $27,000 a year after taxes didn't seem like a lot of lifestyle to Jack – certainly not the lifestyle of a near millionaire! But then Jill reminded him that they both qualified for $25,000 in annual Social Security benefits.

Jack began to relax a bit – until, that is – his tax advisor pointed out that his Social Security benefits would be taxed because the bulk of his income was coming from his 401k (not IRA). Rather than the full $25,000 benefit, he'd end up with just over $21,000 in benefits after taxes. That was – of course – before mandatory means-tested Medicare premiums were deducted from his Social Security check. And unfortunately again - because much of his income would come from his 401k – his means-tested Medicare premiums would be higher than Jill's.

Jill knew that the income she took from her IUL would impact neither – so she would get the full $25,000 Social Security Benefit along with the lowest possible Medicare premium.

At the end of the day, it looked like Jack would have to make do on a bit less than $47,000 a year all in (after taxes) – while Jill would live it up on almost $80,000 a year. Jack was really beginning to question the wisdom of all the people in his life that had been urging and encouraging him to take maximum advantage of the company 401k plan and his employer's generous matching fund policy.

As his questions grew, Jack recalled a time during their working years when Jill had needed to take money out of her IUL for an emergency and had been able to do so without tax or penalty. When Jack had needed money in a similar situation, he was told that if he took it out of his qualified plan, he'd have to pay both tax and penalty.

Not wanting to do so, he had decided instead to put that – rather large expense on a credit card – which took him more than 4 years to pay off – 4 years where he had to do without some of the other niceties of life while he toiled away to pay off the credit card balance. Jill never had to make such a sacrifice when she got the money she needed from her IUL and paid it back on her terms – at her leisure.

Then there was college. Both of their kids went to the same University – at the same time – even had the same major. But Jill – who earned the same amount of income as Jack, qualified for much more need-based student aid than Jack – which meant she paid considerably less for her student's college expenses than Jack had.

Why? Simply because Jill had saved her money in an indexed universal life insurance policy which exempted 100% of her accumulated money as well as her ongoing deposits from the calculations that determine need-based aid eligibility; while Jack's 401k contributions had reduced his aid eligibility. Once again – Jack sacrificed lifestyle during his working years because of the implications of a higher cost for college resulting from his commitment to his 401k.

In fact, those sacrifices spilled over to retirement as much of Jack's ability to save for retirement through accounts outside his 401k were soaked up by the obligations of college for his kids.

Thinking back, Jack also realized the toll financial stress had taken on him as several times over his working life when markets took huge downswings – sapping tens of thousands of dollars from his 401k at a time.

He had even experienced some health challenges because of the financial stress he'd endured. He remembered 2008 and 2009, when the market nearly wiped him out. He also remembered the peace of mind Jill had through it all – claiming that her money contract had never lost a single penny in value to market risk.

Speaking of health – Jack realized that maybe his advisor was right about holding some of his principal in reserve in case of a long-term care need. He had no long-term care insurance – and if he ended up needing that care – he'd have to pay for it out of his own pocket. Jill of course had a benefit built right into her plan, and would be able to draw tax-free money above and beyond her income should she face a similar need.

It was almost more than Jack could take in. Everybody had told him all his life to load up on the company's 401k plan. His employer, his wife, all the trade publications he read, the guy on the radio with the annoying southern accent, his advisor, everybody! How could it have turned out this way?

Jack was no longer looking to live it up in retirement – he was now just hoping to survive it.

To be fair, Jack wasn't exactly going to be living in poverty. With $47,000, he'd get by just fine and be able to do some of the things he'd planned on, but many of his retirement dreams had become retirement nightmares as he adjusted to this new reality.

Jill would continue to live worry-free, just the way she had for the previous 37 years. She didn't have to care what the markets did – what congress did with tax rates – any of it. And with almost $80,000 of tax-free retirement income, she'd surely be able to do more than Jack would.

Perhaps she'd even invite Jack to visit them at their Florida condo when the cold winter weather sets in.

	Jack	Jill
Saving Rate	$500/month + $250 employer match = $750	$500 - 30% in taxes = $350/month
Growth Rate	6.5% (less 1.5% fees/commissions)	6.5% less cost of insurance policy
Timeframe	37 years	37 years
Balance at Retirement	$960,376	$551,901 money contract, $763,349 insurance account

Income in Retirement	$38,415 before tax, $26,890 after	$54,336 tax-free
Social Security	$25,000 less $3,750 in taxes = $21,250	$25,000 – no tax deduction
Total after-tax income	**$48,140**	**$79,336**
Medicare Premiums	Means-tested: could impact Jack for life	Means-tested – Lowest published rate for life
Pre-Retirement Access	Must pay tax plus 10% penalty	Unrestricted, tax & penalty free Access
College	401k Contributions decreased financial aid	Maximum eligible financial aid
Long-term care	pays out-of-pocket	Access to additional benefits
Market Risk	Endured daily	Never a concern
Future Tax Rate Risk	Will endure until end-of-life	Immune forever

I encourage you to reflectively consider what you signed up for when they dangled that 401k or other kind of qualified plan in front of you.

If you've already started, you haven't done a 'bad' thing – you've just done something that you now know may not be in your best long-term interest. Thankfully, you have the option to stop feeding your 401k, and start an indexed universal life insurance policy instead.

If you never started in the first place, perhaps you can avoid Jack's story, get going with your own IUL policy and change your outcome forever.

If your current advisor knows about, and advocates indexed universal life insurance – you're in luck. If not, you need to first decide if you're more committed to your advisor – or your money.

If you're more committed to your money and can't find an advisor who you can trust to lead you through the learning process and construction of a plan that is right for you, I'll do my best to introduce you to a professional in your area who knows and understands these plans inside-out. I work with hundreds all over the country - every day.

The challenge is now yours. You have information that has been withheld from you until now. Will you act – or will you continue to follow the herd?

CHAPTER 28

A Note to Roth-ers

I f you are among the relatively small but growing percentage of Qualified Plan owners who has access to a Roth IRA or a Roth 401k, you've made a better choice than your non-Roth brethren. But your choice is not without its drawbacks.

Let's first look at the good news. The greatest benefit to a Roth plan is that you have immunized your money from future taxation. If you think taxes are on their way up – this is a huge advantage.

You are also able to access your principal contributions (not the growth) prior to age 59-½, without penalty.

There are also no RMD's (Required Minimum Distributions), which means there is no forced taxation on money you may not need for lifestyle.

Finally, distributions taken from Roth plans are not counted as income for determining the taxation of your Social Security benefits – or for calculating your Means-Tested Medicare premiums.

In all, this is a significant basket of benefits compared to a traditional 401k or IRA.

But there's also some not-so-good-news.

You are still in a one-sided partnership with the government. And while your partner has decided you won't need to pay taxes on the balance in your account when its withdrawn, that same government has a way of changing its mind – and your Roth account may look like a juicy T-bone to tax-starved legislators.

Roth plans also have contribution limits that are so restrictive they can only serve in a secondary role – at best - for retirement.

There are also income limitations which can make them completely unavailable to higher income earners.

Roth 401ks and Roth IRA's are better than traditional 401ks, but they're still 'half-a-loaf' compared to what's available through an indexed universal life insurance policy.

CHAPTER 29

A Note to Business Owners and the Self-Employed

f you're a small business owner or self-employed entrepreneur, you have an even more unique opportunity to leverage the power of indexed universal life insurance. Let's look at your personal opportunity first – then what you can achieve with and for your employees.

Leaving money in your business (business equity) exposes that money to three kinds of risk:

Market risk (the risk of your business or industry – in addition to the risk of economy on the whole);

Tax-rate risk (the equity in your business will be taxable at some future unknown rate when taken out); and

Liquidity risk (business equity can be hard and/or expensive to extract from the business).

Taking money out of your business and putting it into a 401k or similar qualified plan accomplishes the goal of getting money out of the business and into your personal account – which is a good thing, and should be a primary objective of all business owners.   But it leaves that 'harvested' money exposed to the exact same three risks – Market Risk, Future Tax-Rate Risk, and Liquidity Risk.

Funding an indexed universal life insurance policy however, both gets money into your personal name, and eliminates all three risks in one fell swoop.

Additionally, the money in your indexed universal life insurance policy is asset-protected from creditors and predators – a valuable benefit for business owners and the self-employed.

But IUL presents you with another – very interesting opportunity. As you build equity in your policy's money contract, you can 'loan' money from the policy's insurance account - to your business.

When your business money borrows from you – it repays that money to you – with interest of course. Not only do those payments go back into your account (rather than to a third-party bank or lender), it gets even more interesting when you charge a higher interest rate to the business for the money you lend it.

If the law in your state allows you to charge 15% interest on money you loan your business – and that is 10% more than you'd pay a bank – you suddenly have an opportunity to move money from your business into your personal, IUL account where it can grow tax-deferred, and is accessible tax-free.

That interest expense is deductible to the business, which lowers the tax liability of the business' profits.

So – you can have the benefit of money making its way into your IUL account; that is tax-deductible to your business; which grows tax-deferred; and is accessible from your policy tax-free.

The interest you collect from the business is taxable income to you personally (less the internal interest charge in your policy), but if you would have otherwise taken that money out of the business as personal income – it would have been taxed anyway.

Now however, it is 'passive' income rather than 'earned' income, and is exempt from the 15.3% self-employment tax. That means that each dollar you move to your personal ownership via this strategy is worth 15.3% more to you than a dollar paid to you by your business in salary or distribution.

In summary, the interest that's going into your IUL account is:

a. Tax-Deductible to the business

b. Grows tax-deferred in your IUL policy,

c. Is accessible tax-free via policy loans, and

d. Will pass on income tax-free to others.

Not a bad deal!

Finally, IUL can also be a great way to retain and reward key employees. While a 401k plan will likely be viewed as a valuable employee benefit, it's portability means it does not serve as an employee retention tool. An IUL plan offered to employees however, can serve as an excellent employee benefit as well as an employee retention strategy for the business.

Many small business owners use money that would otherwise be paid in 401k matching contributions – to fund (or partially fund) IUL policies for key employees. Since IUL is not a qualified plan, you have much more flexibility to 'make the rules' regarding who can participate, and to what degree.

Unlike the 401k, you can 'discriminate' between employees/groups of employees – which can make IUL a bona fide recruiting and/or retention tool.

You will need competent professional guidance in constructing an insurance based retirement plan that meets your needs and is compliant, but more and more employers are finding great business benefits in doing so.

CHAPTER 30

A Note to the Reader

I ndexed Universal Life Insurance is (roughly) a 20-year old product. It is a vastly different animal than its better-known cousins - Whole Life or Variable Universal Life.

As the most consumer-friendly product the industry has ever offered, it is by far the growth leader among permanent life insurance products – for all the reasons we've just discovered and detailed.

Not all insurance companies offer an IUL product. Of those who do, not all products are good, nor are all insurance companies. For sure, not all insurance agents know this product and how to properly structure it to deliver the outcomes we have discussed here.

For those who are inclined to conduct their own independent research, I can assure you that before your finger leaves the 'search' button on Google – you will be bombarded with negative information about life insurance – including the Indexed Universal Life variety.

Some of it will come from media fringe-dwellers who are hopelessly ignorant about life insurance in general. Some of it will come from inside the industry itself. Most of it will come from a very well-organized, aristocratic, entrenched, and limitlessly funded, Wall Street Cartel – along with their surrogates in the financial press who derive advertising dollars and in turn - provide them cover.

And it's not hard to understand why. Walk into a run-of-the-mill brokerage or advisory firm, or even one of the big national brands - and tell them you want a product that:

- Offers guaranteed protection from downside market risk and market-driven upside growth potential,

- Grows tax-deferred – and is accessible tax-free,

- Will pay a large, tax-free sum of money to your heirs,

- Will safely generate more income per dollar of account balance than anything else going,

- Is immune from all future tax-rate increases,

- Will qualify you for more need-based college financial aid,

- Won't (on its own) trigger the taxation of your Social Security benefits or drive up Medicare premiums,

- Offers a separate, premium-free benefit for qualifying health or long-term care events, and

- Has low – even disappearing fees.

See what happens. See if they don't break out in uncontrollable laughter or call the 'white padded van' to come pick you up.

The Truth is - they can't compete!

But just as traditional cab companies have done everything they can to undermine higher-service, lower-cost upstarts like Uber and Lyft – the Wall Street Cartel will protect its turf to the death – yours!

Navigating your way through the noise will be tough. So will finding a competent insurance professional. But at least you now have the blueprint to guide you through the process.

Like all tough journeys, the reward will be worth it. I am not a celebrity, nor am I hard to find or get ahold of. If I can help in any way – I hope you'll reach out. I know the best insurance companies, the best products, and the best advisors.

Unless you are a friend, family member, or personal referral, I will never sell you anything, but I will give you the benefit of all the knowledge and experience I've accumulated over the years. Because at the end of the day, mine is a crusade to change the way America saves money – and builds wealth.

89604664R00090

Made in the USA
Lexington, KY
31 May 2018